SECOND EDITION

Workbook **4**

SUPER MINDS

Herbert Puchta · Peter Lewis-Jones · Günter Gerngross · Catherine Zgouras

CAMBRIDGE
UNIVERSITY PRESS

Contents

Well done, Ben and Lucy!

1 Look at the pictures and letters. Write the words.

1 greathophopr
photographer

2 routjailns

3 pcomeiorhn

4 dabn

5 mogded scar

6 llerro astcore

7 bgi lhewe

8 robotduuan

9 ymrao

2 Read and write the words.
1 He writes stories for newspapers. _____journalist_____
2 He's the most important man in town. _____
3 She takes photos. _____
4 Four fairground rides. _____

_____

3 What is your favourite fairground ride?

_____

1 Match the questions and answers.

1 Are you eleven?

2 What's your favourite colour?

3 When do you get up in the mornings?

4 Where do you go on your holidays?

5 Who is your best friend?

6 Do you like going on adventures with Ben?

7 Does Ben ever make you angry?

8 Is it fun being an Explorer?

a Yes, it is.

b Ben, of course.

c Yes, I do.

d Blue, definitely.

e Sometimes, when he's scared of silly things.

f About 7 o'clock.

g No, I'm ten.

h I go to the beach.

2 Complete the questions.

1 _____How_____ old are you?

2 _____ do you live?

3 _____ you got any brothers or sisters?

4 _____ your favourite colour red?

5 _____ your school got a uniform?

6 _____ is your favourite lesson?

7 _____ do you get home from school?

8 _____ you tell your best friend everything?

3 Answer the questions in Activity 2 about you.

1 _____

2 _____

3 _____

4 _____

5 _____

6 _____

7 _____

8 _____

1 🛡 **Remember the song. Write the words in order.**

fun / Here / they / ~~The~~ / come / and /
Adventure / and / Lucy / ~~Explorers~~ / Ben

The Explorers
_____
_____
_____

stars / Ben / are / Here / The / and /
Action / they / Lucy / Explorers

_____
_____
_____
_____

2 🛡 **Is it Ben or Lucy in the song? Write the sentences in the correct box.**

I find the treasure.   I like adventure.
I love exploring things.   I'm not scared of anything.

_____
_____
_____

_____
_____
_____

3 **Answer the questions and check your answers.**

ARE YOU AN
EXPLORER?

1 Do you like adventure? _____

2 Do you like exploring things? _____

3 Do you like exciting things? _____

4 Are you scared of anything? _____

KEY

Q 1–3: yes = 1 point, no = 0 points
Q 4: no = 1 point, yes = 0 points

4 points: You're a true Explorer, just like Ben and Lucy.

3 points: You're nearly an Explorer.

1–2 points: You aren't an Explorer at the moment.

0 points: You aren't really an Explorer.

1 🎧 **001** **What did Emma do at the party? Listen and tick** ✓.

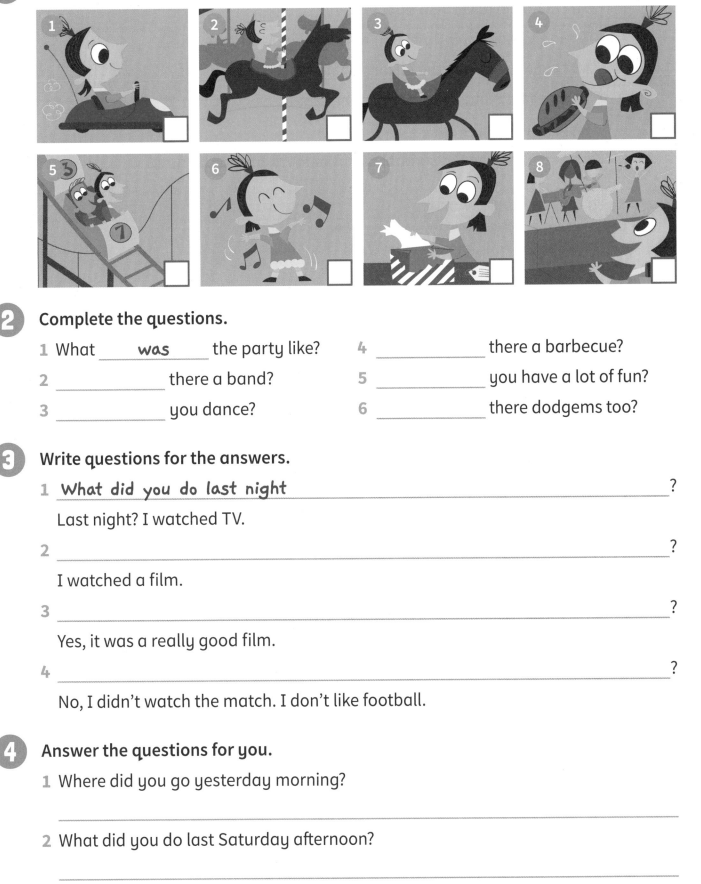

2 **Complete the questions.**

1 What _____was_____ the party like?

2 _____ there a band?

3 _____ you dance?

4 _____ there a barbecue?

5 _____ you have a lot of fun?

6 _____ there dodgems too?

3 **Write questions for the answers.**

1 What did you do last night _____ ?

Last night? I watched TV.

2 _____ ?

I watched a film.

3 _____ ?

Yes, it was a really good film.

4 _____ ?

No, I didn't watch the match. I don't like football.

4 **Answer the questions for you.**

1 Where did you go yesterday morning?

_____

2 What did you do last Saturday afternoon?

_____

1 Read the story *The map* again. Then put the sentences in order.

[ ] Mr Davidson tells them about a king.

[1] The children tell Mr Davidson about their adventure.

[ ] Mr Davidson shows the children a map.

[ ] Mr Davidson finds a symbol on the statue.

[ ] Horax phones Zelda.

[ ] The children see the symbol and read a rhyme on the map.

2 Read and write the words.

go   rhyme   quiz   is   ~~know~~   find

Study the map, so then you (1) ____know____

The places where you have to (2) _____.

When you get there, look and (3) _____

A line like this to make a (4) _____.

The lines together make a (5) _____

To tell you where the treasure (6) _____.

3 The pictures on the map tell Ben and Lucy where to look.
Look, guess and write sentences. Use words from the box.

school   library   lake   station   ~~museum~~   concert hall
castle   statue   art gallery   restaurant   planetarium   zoo

1

I think they have
to find a museum.

2

_____
_____

3

_____
_____

4

_____
_____

5

_____
_____

6

_____
_____

1 Colour the bricks to make sentences. Write in the missing words.

1	_Does_ your	you go on	in a band?
2	_____ your parents	TV	yesterday?
3	Where _____	brother play	the weekend?
4	_____ you watch	you do at	Spanish?
5	_____ did	speak	holiday last summer?

2 Match the rhyming words.

1 noise   a trees
2 rhyme   b snow
3 shoe   c boys
4 toe   d time
5 cheese   e glue

3 🎧 002 **Listen, say and check your answers.**

4 🛡 **Imagine you went to a theme park. What did you see and do? Read. Then write about you and draw.**

I saw a big roller coaster. I went on
a roundabout. It was fun. Then I ...

_____

_____

_____

1 In the museum

1 Complete the words. Then look and match.

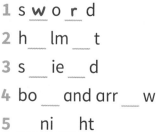
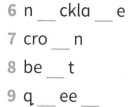

1 s w o r d
2 h __ lm __ t
3 s __ ie __ d
4 bo __ and arr __ w
5 __ ni __ ht

6 n __ ckla __ e
7 cro __ n
8 be __ t
9 q __ ee __
10 b __ a __ elet

2 Look, read and number the sentences.

a **3** She's wearing a dress, a crown and two bracelets.

b ☐ He's wearing a helmet. He's carrying a shield and a bow and arrow.

c ☐ She's wearing a dress with a belt, a crown and a bracelet.

d ☐ He's carrying his helmet. He's wearing his sword on his belt.

3 Imagine you are a queen or a knight. What are you wearing? Write sentences.

I'm a _____.

I'm wearing a _____.

1 Look and write the sentences under the pictures.

> I must drink more water.   I mustn't touch my sister's things.
> I must spend time with my grandparents.   I mustn't eat too much ice cream.
> I must do my homework.   ~~I mustn't run in the living room.~~

I mustn't run in
the living room.

2 Complete with *must* or *mustn't* and a word from the box.

> shout   keep   use   ~~wear~~   drink   buy

1 I ___must___ ___wear___ a helmet when I ride my bike.

2 I _____ _____ in the house when my baby brother is sleeping.

3 I _____ _____ water from the lake. It isn't clean.

4 I _____ _____ the dog on his lead. I don't want him to chase cats.

5 I _____ _____ a new T-shirt. I've got too many already!

6 I _____ _____ my camera here. The sign says 'No photos'.

3 What must or mustn't you do at home or at school? Write four sentences: two with *must* and two with *mustn't*.

I mustn't be late for school.

1 Remember the song. Match.

1 listen quietly

2 take photos

3 write about the trip

must

mustn't

4 use my mobile phone

5 shout

6 run

2 Complete the song about you. Then draw a picture.

There's a museum trip tomorrow
To learn our history,
But now I'm thinking about the things
My teacher said to me.
I must _____.
I mustn't _____.
I must _____.
I mustn't _____.

3 Write the phrases from the box in the correct column.
Then add one more to each column.

be polite   make noise   help my classmates   eat sweets
listen to music on my phone   be on time   make a mess   help my teacher

In class, I must	In class, I mustn't
be polite	

1 Circle the correct word.

1 Please help <u>Bob</u>. Help (him) / he.

2 Please show the photo to <u>Jenna</u>. Show **she** / **her** the photo.

3 Please write <u>Ruby and me</u> an email. Write **us** / **we** an email.

4 Tell the story to <u>Frank and Amy</u>. Tell **they** / **them** the story.

5 Buy a new dress for <u>Mia</u>. Buy **her** / **she** a new dress.

6 Please give the pen to <u>Jack</u>. Give **he** / **him** the pen.

2 Change the sentences.

1 Don't show the letter to Joel and Frank.

   <u>Don't show the letter to them.</u>

2 Don't take the oranges!

   _____

3 Please don't shout at Bella and me.

   _____

4 Please don't give any bananas to Ella.

   _____

3 Write two more sentences using direct or indirect objects.

1 <u>**Please feed the dog and cat**</u>. Please feed them.

2 _____. Look at us.

3 _____. Don't eat it.

1 Read the story *The knight* again. Write *t* (true) or *f* (false).

1 Someone is trying to hurt Lucy and Ben with a shield. **f**

2 The knight comes after them. ☐

3 The knight finds Lucy and Ben. ☐

4 The knight falls down the stairs. ☐

5 Lucy and Ben find a rhyme on the knight's sword. ☐

6 The knight was Zelda. ☐

2 Read and write the words.

chase   queen   children   knight   ~~dressing~~   going

To: zelda@megamail.co.uk   Subject: I have a plan!

Hi Zelda,

I'm **(1)** ___dressing___ up as the **(2)** _____ ! When the **(3)** _____ come into the museum, I'm **(4)** _____ to scare them. Then I'm going to **(5)** _____ them. You can be the **(6)** _____ .

Horax

3 Look and match. Then complete the sentences.

1 The dinosaur _is from the Nature Museum_ .

2 The owl _____ .

3 The motorbike _____ .

4 The shield _____ .

5 The plane _____ .

6 The knight _____ .

1 🎧 003 **Listen and write the missing words. Then say with a friend.**

Tim: Look out!

Sue: What was that?

Tim: The tree. It just fell.

Sue: Wow! _____
_____ _____!

Liam: What am I going to buy you for your birthday?

Kim: _____ _____
_____ _____!

Liam: What?

Kim: Nothing! That's what you bought me last year!

2 **Match the sounds and colour the squares yellow or brown.**

yellow	brown	bow and arrow	crown
know	window	how	town
show	now	flower	snow

3 🎧 004 **Listen, say and check your answers.**

1 🛡 Read Aunt Jill's stories again. Complete the sentences.

1 The family and their dog were walking by ___the river___ .

2 Grandpa saved the dog because it wasn't good at _____ .

3 Jill painted her brother's _____ .

4 Jill put the wrong _____ on the table.

5 Grandpa always _____ .

6 One day Grandpa forgot Jill and left her in a _____ .

2 Write t (true) or f (false).

1 Family stories are about dogs. ☐ f

2 The dog was in danger because it was a bad swimmer. ☐

3 Grandpa helped the dog get out of the water. ☐

4 Jill dressed her brother in green. ☐

5 The lady didn't like her tea. ☐

6 Jill didn't notice her dad wasn't in the shop. ☐

3 🖐 🛡 Read the story again and think. Colour the circles green for yes or red for no.

◯ We can learn a lot about our family history when we listen to family stories.

◯ Family stories are boring.

1 Peter is telling Sophie about his week. What did he do with these people? Listen and write a letter in each box. There is one example.

his grandpa **e**

his teacher

his cousins

his mother

his sister

his friends

a EGYPT PROJECT

b

c

d SUGAR FLOUR BUTTER

e MUSEUM

f ANCIENT EGYPT

g

h

TIMELINES >>>>>>

1 Read the text and answer the questions.

Timelines show different events in the right order. They help us to understand history. Timelines tell us what happened and how much time there was between important events. Timelines don't have big texts to read, but they always have the important events and the dates. Many timelines also have pictures. Timelines can also show people's lives, explain life cycles of plants and animals, and show events in stories. You could even make a timeline about your holiday.

1 Are timelines used only in history? _____No, they aren't._____

2 Do timelines show events in any order? _____

3 Do timelines have big texts? _____

4 What two things do timelines always have? _____

5 What else can timelines have? _____

6 What can timelines explain? _____

2 Read the text and complete the timeline with the dates and important events.

Thousands of years ago our world was different. There wasn't any reading and writing. Learning things was difficult. But in 3200 BCE, writing was invented. People started to write about important events in history. The Roman alphabet was invented in 1600 BCE. And when was paper first made? It was in 100 CE. The first paper was made in China. The oldest printed book was made in 800 CE, in China too. It was printed from pieces of wood. Books made learning things easier. In 1088 CE, the first university was started in Italy, so people could learn about difficult things. But there weren't many books. A man called Gutenberg invented a printing machine in 1440 CE. After that lots of books were made quickly. Now there are millions of books and it's easy to read and learn.

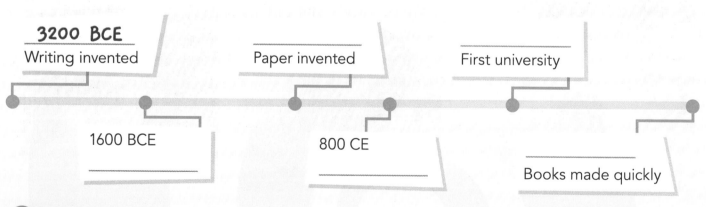

3200 BCE
Writing invented

_____
Paper invented

_____
First university

1600 BCE
_____

800 CE
_____

_____
Books made quickly

3 🛡 **Look at the timeline. Then complete the text.**

700 – the first knights

1023 – Knights Hospitaller

1348 – Order of the Garter

1400s – knights gave money to the king

Today – people who do something important are made knights

A knight was a person who worked for the king. Usually it was someone who had a lot of money. This is because knights needed a horse, a sword and a shield. These were very expensive! Men first became knights in **(1)** ____700____. They helped the king and the king gave them land. Knights were important people because they had a lot of money and land. Later, the knights made their own groups. One of the first groups were the **(2)** _____, who started in 1023. They helped people who were ill.

In 1348, King Edward III of England started a famous group of knights: the **(3)** _____. Then, in the **(4)** _____, many knights gave money to the king so they didn't have to help him. The king used this money to get other people to help him.

Today, people are still knights, but they don't ride horses. It is just a special name. It is given to people who do **(5)** _____. Men are 'Sir' and women are 'Dame'. Bill Gates, who started Microsoft, is a knight. Angelina Jolie, the actress, is a dame.

4 🛡 **Imagine you are a king or queen. Make a timeline of people you have made a knight or dame. Write why they have the title.**

2008 Dame Rihanna for helping the poor

_____   _____
_____   _____
_____   _____

_____   _____
_____   _____
_____   _____

1 Match the questions and answers.

1 When did you leave the museum?

2 What did you do outside?

3 Did you go back in the morning?

4 So what did you do?

5 Did you like it outside?

6 Are you going to go out again?

a No, I didn't. The window was closed.

b I don't think so. Mr Benson said, 'I mustn't forget to close the windows.'

c Three nights ago when Mr Benson forgot to close a window.

d I met another cat and we hunted rats.

e Yes, it was great.

f I waited and the next night someone opened the window.

2 Look at Activity 1. Underline the mistakes. Then write the correct sentences.

One night Mr Benson <u>left a door open</u>. The Egyptian cat got out of its glass case. Outside, it met a dog. When the Egyptian cat wanted to get back in, the door was locked. She waited and two nights later someone opened a window. She went back into her glass case.

One night, Mr Benson left a window open.

3 Imagine that a different exhibit escaped. Write what happened.

• Which exhibit escaped?

• What did it do outside?

• When did it go back to the museum?

One day, Mr Benson left the window open again. The

What do I know? 1 Look and draw lines to make sentences.

1 Give

us	the	ball	yesterday, please.
them	a	shoes	tomorrow, please.
me	an	ball	now, please.

2 You

aren't	make	silence	in the museum.
mustn't	be	photos	in the shop.
must	take	a noise	in the zoo.

3 You

must	brush	your hair	before bed.
have	wash	you face	after bed.
mustn't	dry	your teeth	in bed.

BIG QUESTION How can we learn about the past?

2 Read and write two more.

To learn about the past, we can visit museums, _____, _____.

About me! 3 Read. Then write about you and draw.

I talk to my grandparents to learn about the past. They tell me about the 1960s. In the 1960s, ...

2 The world around us

1 Complete the words. Then look and match.

1 i **s** l a **n** d   3 f _ _ _ _ d   5 _ _ t _ _   7 m _ _ _ _ _ a _ _ _

2 l _ _ e   4 v _ _ _ _ _ g _   6 _ v _ r   8 f _ _ _ _ _ t

2 Complete the dialogues with words from Activity 1.

1 A: Can we swim to that ____island____ in the middle of the lake?

  B: No, you can't. But look, we can all go on that boat.

2 A: I can see some lights there. Is that a town?

  B: No, there are only a few houses. It's a _____.

3 A: Let's go through the trees.

  B: No, I think we should stay on the _____. It's safer.

4 A: How can we get across the _____?

  B: Look, there's a bridge.

3 Think about your perfect countryside place. What does it have? Write.

There's a big lake.

_____

_____

1 Find and write the four sentences.

itwasalovelydaysojaneandpollywantedtohaveapicnicalltheirfamilylovedswimminginthelakebecausethewaterwaswarmtheywalkedthroughthefieldsbutthenitstartedtoraintheyrantothecarandtheirdadtookthemhome

1 It was a lovely day, so Jane and Polly wanted to have a picnic.

2 _____

3 _____

4 _____

2 Join the sentences with *and*, *but*, *so* and *because*.

1 There are fields near our village. People love having picnics there.

   There are fields near our village and people love having picnics there.

2 It started to rain. We went home.

   _____

3 John went to the USA. He stayed in Chicago.

   _____

4 Kate liked visiting her uncle. It took two hours by car.

   _____

5 The film was boring. We left the cinema.

   _____

6 Don't go across that old bridge. It's dangerous.

   _____

3 Write four sentences about you. Use *and*, *but*, *so* and *because*.

   I like watching football and ... I like watching tennis, but ...

   _____

   _____

1 🛡 **Remember the song. Complete the verses with the words from the box.**

but ~~swam~~ because fished so climbed

We (1) ___swam___ in the river

(2) _____ it was so hot.

We (3) _____ up the mountain
And reached the top.

We (4) _____ in a little lake.

(5) _____ we didn't catch a thing,

(6) _____ we built a boat from wood
And sailed around like kings.

2 🛡 **Complete the song with your own ideas and then draw a picture.**

We went to _____

And _____

We _____

Because _____

We saw _____

And _____

We _____

But we didn't _____

1 Look at the photo album. What could Beth and Sam do 40 years ago? What couldn't they do? Write sentences with the words from the box.

> ride   drive   run   jump   climb   ~~fly~~

Forty years ago …

1 Beth _____could fly_____ a plane.

2 Sam _____ a marathon.

3 Beth _____ a mountain.

4 Sam _____ out of a plane.

5 Beth _____ a car.

6 Sam _____ an elephant.

2 What can you do now that you couldn't do when you were younger? Write sentences.

When I was three, I couldn't read and write.

_____

_____

_____

_____

1 🛡 **Remember the story** *At the restaurant*. **Write** *t* **(true) or** *f* **(false).**

1 They read the map before lunch. **f**

2 The map has pictures they have to find. ☐

3 The red lions aren't in the zoo. ☐

4 Grandpa loses the map. ☐

5 Lucy has the map. ☐

6 The waiter wanted the map. ☐

2 🛡 **Complete the waiter's diary entry.**

> angry   in the boy's pocket   some bread   children   ~~old man~~
> had soup   a map   red lions at the zoo   a lion   was a menu

Today there was an **(1)** _____old man_____ in the restaurant. He was
with two **(2)** _____ . They **(3)** _____ for lunch.
When I took the soup, I saw **(4)** _____ on the table. I wanted
to know about it, so I took **(5)** _____ to their table. One child
said the next picture on the map was **(6)** _____ , but the
other one said that you don't find **(7)** _____ . I took the map,
but when I looked at it in the kitchen, I saw that it **(8)** _____ .
I think the old man took the map and put the menu **(9)** _____ .
I was very **(10)** _____ !

3 ✋ 🛡 **Read the story again and think. Draw** 😃 **or** 😫 **.**

◯ We should spend time with our family.

◯ We should only spend time with our friends.

1 🎧 006 **Listen and write the missing words. Then say with a friend.**

1

Jen: Mr Price, this is for your new house.

Mr Price: _____ _____
_____ plant!
Thank you! That's very kind.

2

Dawn: Did you see those two men in the car?

Dan: Yes, what about them?

Dawn: _____ _____
_____ _____
_____ them.

Dan: What do you mean?

Dawn: One had a T-shirt and shorts, and the other had a big winter coat and boots!

2 **Match to make sentences. Then circle the silent consonants.**

1 The (k)ni(gh)t's ——————————— a knows about volcanoes.

2 Please write b answer.

3 The scientist c got a s(w)ord.

4 The rhinos live d listen to the teacher.

5 That's the wrong e a rhyme in your notebooks.

6 At school you must f on an island.

3 🎧 007 **Listen, say and check your answers.**

1 🎧 008 **Listen and write. There is one example.**

KATE'S BIRTHDAY PARTY

Number of people at the party: **three**

Book was about: _____

Her favourite present: _____

Time they went out: _____

Where they went: _____

Who played a scary trick: _____

2 **Now write the story. Use the pictures and the sentences in Activity 1 to help you.**

It was Kate's birthday. She had a small party with her sister and friend.

_____

_____

_____

_____

3 🛡 **Imagine you went on a night walk. What did you see?**

_____

_____

_____

1 **Read the text and choose the best answer.**

Example

Jim: **What did you do on Saturday?**

Polly: (A) We visited a small village.

B Yes, I did.

C It was fun.

Questions

1 Jim: **Did you have lunch there?**

Polly: A Yes, we do.

B Yes, we did.

C At half past one.

2 Jim: **What did you have for lunch?**

Polly: A I had a good time.

B I have a tomato sandwich.

C I had soup and some bread.

3 Jim: **Did you see anything interesting?**

Polly: A I see my friends every day.

B I saw a lake and a mountain.

C Swimming.

4 Jim: **Did you climb the mountain?**

Polly: A No, because it was too hot.

B So we went to the lake.

C And we went fishing.

5 Jim: **Was the lake big?**

Polly: A Yes, that's a good idea.

B Yes, it was.

C Was it?

6 Jim: **Are you going to the village again?**

Polly: A Yes, I did. It was very beautiful.

B Yes, and you can come too.

C Yes, it is.

Maps and satellites

1 Complete the sentences with the words from the box.

continent   country   city   ~~city centre~~   satellites   satellite images

1 There is a big park in the _city centre_ . We go there after school.

2 _____ help meteorologists see if dangerous weather is coming.

3 I think living in a _____ is exciting because you can do many things.

4 Asia is the biggest _____ on our planet.

5 _____ help us talk to people all over the world.

6 Australia is a very big _____ . It's one of the biggest islands on our planet.

2 Read the text. Tick ✓ the correct sentences.

A satellite is an object that goes around a planet. There are two different kinds of satellite: natural satellites and artificial satellites. The moon is a natural satellite. It goes around the Earth. Other planets have natural satellites too. Artificial satellites are made by people and then put in space. Some artificial satellites help us by taking photos of space. They tell us what is happening in space and what is happening to the Earth. Other satellites help us communicate with people all over the world. Weather satellites tell us what the weather will be like, so we can get ready for bad weather. The biggest satellite is the International Space Station. Astronauts from all over the world live and work on this satellite. The astronauts collect information and send it back to Earth. Satellites use energy from the sun. They collect sunlight and turn it into electricity. Today there are thousands of satellites in space.

1 Natural satellites do not give us any information about space.   ✓

2 The moon is an artificial satellite.   ☐

3 Satellites help us talk to people in different parts of the world.   ☐

4 Astronauts live and work on the biggest artificial satellite.   ☐

5 Satellites use other satellites to make electricity.   ☐

3 Look at these satellite images. Write what they show.

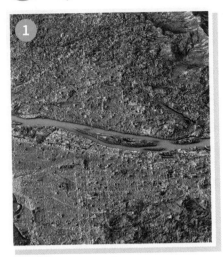

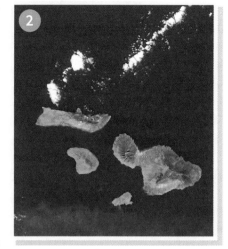

a river

_____

_____

_____

_____

_____

4 Imagine you have a satellite image. What places does it show? Write and then draw a picture of it.

My satellite picture shows _____

_____

_____

_____

_____

_____

_____

_____

1 Match the questions and answers.

1 What do you prefer doing in your free time, Isabel?

2 What activities do you like doing outdoors?

3 And when you are at home, what do you like doing?

4 Do you spend a lot of time on the Internet?

5 What about being in town? Do you like that?

6 Do you like going to shops?

a I love walking, watching birds and helping in the garden.

b Not very much because there are too many cars and it's noisy.

c Yes, I use it every day to look for information and I write emails.

d I love reading a lot. When I have a good book, I can't stop. I never watch TV.

e Yes, I do. Sometimes I go with Mum and we have lots of fun.

f When the weather is nice, I prefer being outdoors. When it rains, I love staying at home.

2 Look at Activity 1. <u>Underline</u> the mistakes. Then write the correct sentences.

Isabel is very much an outdoor person. She <u>likes riding her bike</u>. She also likes listening to birds and sleeping in the garden. When the weather is nice, she loves being at home. She watches a lot of TV. She never uses a computer and she doesn't send emails. Isabel doesn't like being in town very much. She thinks that there are too many people.

She loves walking.

_____

_____

_____

_____

_____

3 Write about your free time.

I'm an outdoor person.

1 Colour the bricks to make sentences. Write in the missing words.

1	He liked the book	was young	they saw a snake.
2	They were scared	and	speak English at all.
3	When Grandma	two I _____	she _____ run really fast.
4	When I was	_____	went to bed.
5	She was tired	_____ she	he __couldn't__ stop reading it!

2 **Read and think.**

BIG QUESTION What do we know about the outside world?

Then write three more.

In the outside world, there are mountains, rivers, _____,
_____ and _____.

 3 **Read. Then write about you and draw.**

I love climbing mountains because
it's fun. I don't like swimming, so I
don't go to lakes.

_____
_____
_____
_____

3 Danger!

1 Complete the words.

1 f i r e
2 fl _ _ d
3 _ m b _ l _ n c _
4 p _ l _ c _ c _ r
5 p _ r _ m _ d _ c

6 f _ _ r _ f _ ght _ r
7 p _ l _ c _ _ ff _ c _ r
8 f _ r _ _ ng _ n _
9 _ m _ rg _ ncy s _ rv _ c _ s

2 Complete the diagram with the words from Activity 1.

EMERGENCY SERVICES

PEOPLE

DANGERS
fire

VEHICLES

3 Read and complete with the words from Activity 2.

A few days ago, I was on my way to school and I saw smoke. It was coming out of a house. I had my mobile phone, so I called the **(1)** __emergency services__ . Five minutes later, a big red **(2)** _____ came down the road. It stopped and four **(3)** _____ got out. It was really exciting. They started to fight the **(4)** _____ and there was water everywhere! It was like a **(5)** _____ . Then an **(6)** _____ arrived with two **(7)** _____ , but there wasn't anyone in the house, so they went back to the hospital. Finally, two **(8)** _____ arrived. 'Do you live here?' one of them asked me. 'No, I don't,' I said, 'but I called the emergency services.' 'That's good,' the other said, 'but you should be at school now. What school do you go to?' 'Castle Park,' I answered. 'OK, we can take you,' one of them said … and I got a ride in a **(9)** _____ !

1 **Complete with the correct form of the verbs.**

Yesterday at 11 o'clock in the park, …

1 Tim _____was riding_____ (ride) his bike.

2 Mr Brown _____ (read) a newspaper.

3 Ian and Ruth _____ (play) football.

4 my dog _____ (chase) a ball.

5 Sara _____ (run).

6 Mr and Mrs Smith _____ (walk) their dog.

2 **Look at the picture. Write sentences with the verbs from the box.**

talk

fight

try

sing

~~watch~~

Yesterday at 8 o'clock, …

1 Mum and Dad _were watching_____ TV.

2 my brother _____.

3 my sister _____ on the phone.

4 the dog and the cat _____.

5 and I _____ to do my homework!

3 **What were you and your family doing yesterday at 8 o'clock? Write sentences.**

1 _I was reading a book._____

2 _____

3 _____

4 _____

1 Remember the song. Complete the sentences. Then match.

1 She ___was swimming___ in the sea.

2 The shark _____ next to her.

3 She _____ by the lake.

4 She _____ down the street.

2 Complete these sentences. Use your imagination. Write what happened.

1 I was swimming in the lake. _____

2 I was running in the park. _____

3 I was walking to school. _____

3 Write a verse using one of your ideas from Activity 2. Try to make it rhyme. Then draw a picture.

I was _____

_____

_____

_____ .

1 Match the questions and answers.

1 What was Jack doing at 7 o'clock?
2 What were you and Sue doing?
3 What was the cat doing?
4 What was Jill doing at 8 o'clock?
5 What were you doing?
6 What were Bill and Liz doing?

a I was doing my homework.
b He was playing computer games.
c They were playing cards.
d It was sleeping.
e We were watching TV.
f She was listening to music.

2 Look and write questions for the answers.

a Grandma   b Grandpa   c Nathan and Jacob   d Dad

1 What **was Grandma doing at 3 o'clock** ?
She was gardening.

2 _____, Grandpa?
I was reading a book.

3 _____?
They were riding their bikes.

4 _____?
He was cooking.

3 Answer the questions about you and your family on Sunday.

1 What were you doing at 6 o'clock? I was sleeping.
2 Were you playing at 7 o'clock?
3 What was your dad doing at 8 o'clock?
4 Was your mum cooking at 9 o'clock?
5 What were your family doing at 10 o'clock?

1 Read the story *The man in the car* again. Put the lines in order.

- [ ] Ben's grandfather puts out the fire.
- [ ] A fast motorbike goes past them.
- [ ] Lucy tells the operator where they are.
- [1] Ben's grandfather sees a person in an accident.
- [ ] The ambulance arrives.
- [ ] Ben's grandfather pulls the man out of the car.
- [ ] Ben's grandfather gets out of the car.

2 Read and circle.

1 Why does Ben's grandfather say, 'Stay in the car, please'?
   a Because he wants Lucy to talk to the operator.
   (b) Because it's too dangerous for them.

2 Why does the operator ask Lucy about the house number?
   a Because she wants to know where Lucy lives.
   b Because she's going to send an ambulance there.

3 Why does Ben's grandfather say to the man, 'Quick. We must get you out'?
   a Because the man's leg hurts.
   b Because it's dangerous to stay in the car after the accident.

4 Why does Ben's grandfather say, 'Don't go so fast'?
   a Because the man on the motorbike is a dangerous driver.
   b Because the man on the motorbike is making them wet.

3 Complete the summary with the words.

> motorbike   fire extinguisher   flood   fire engine   ~~emergency services~~

Lucy calls the **(1)** __emergency services__. She tells the operator that her friend's grandpa has got a **(2)** _____. The operator tells her she mustn't get out of the car. She must wait for the ambulance and the **(3)** _____. The ambulance arrives and the paramedic helps the man. The man wasn't driving fast, but his car went into the **(4)** _____. But the man on the **(5)** _____ was going too fast. Grandpa thinks he knows who the man on the motorbike is.

1 🎧 009 **Listen and write the missing words. Then say with a friend.**

SMASH!

Zak: Where are you going?

Alien: Back to my planet.

Zak: _____ _____

_____ _____

_____?

Alien: Of course you can.

Zak: Great, but I need to be back for tea at 6 o'clock.

May: There was an accident outside our house last night. We were watching TV and _____

_____ _____

_____ loud noise. I ran to the window and saw two cars.

Liam: Did you call the police?

May: No, I didn't because I could see that no-one was hurt … and one of them was a police car!

2 **Look and complete the words.**

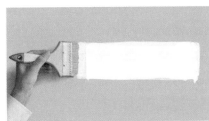

1 kn **ight**

2 wh_____

3 l_____ning

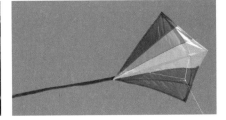

4 midn_____

5 firef_____er

6 k_____

3 🎧 010 **Listen, say and check your answers.**

1 Read Aroon's story again. Circle the correct word.

1 Bejak was Aroon's **dad / (donkey)**.

2 Aroon and his dad wanted to cook **wood / food** for the family.

3 **Aroon / Bejak** became very nervous.

4 Aroon and his family looked for the donkey **on the beach / in the hills**.

5 The donkey ran away because **a tsunami was / dogs were** coming.

6 Aroon's family was **safe / in danger** at the top of the hill.

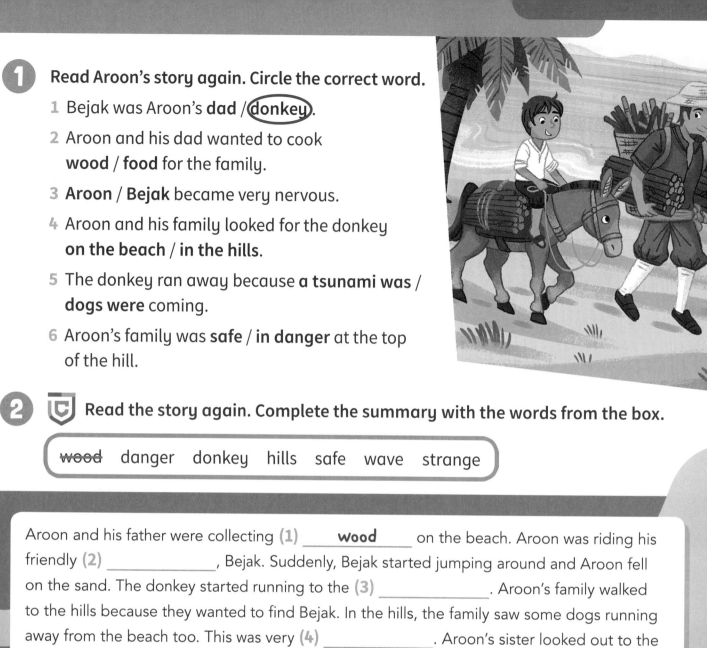

2 Read the story again. Complete the summary with the words from the box.

~~wood~~   danger   donkey   hills   safe   wave   strange

Aroon and his father were collecting **(1) _____wood_____** on the beach. Aroon was riding his friendly **(2) _____**, Bejak. Suddenly, Bejak started jumping around and Aroon fell on the sand. The donkey started running to the **(3) _____**. Aroon's family walked to the hills because they wanted to find Bejak. In the hills, the family saw some dogs running away from the beach too. This was very **(4) _____**. Aroon's sister looked out to the sea. It was a long way out. Suddenly a big strong **(5) _____** came back towards the beach and broke many houses and trees. It also killed many people. Aroon's family found Bejak at the top of the hill. They were all **(6) _____** thanks to their donkey because animals know when there is **(7) _____** from the sea and always go to higher ground.

3 Read the story again and think. Colour the circles green for *yes* or red for *no*.

◯ Some animals are bad.   ◯ Animals and nature can help you.

1 Look and read. Choose the correct words and write them on the lines.

a hut

a hotel

a snorkel

a sandcastle

1 This is a building. You stay here when you are on holiday. ___a hotel___

2 This is very cold. You eat it and it tastes sweet. _____

3 You can breathe under water with this. _____

4 This is a very big wave. It is very dangerous. _____

5 This is a small building. It can be a house or a shop. _____

6 Children like to build this on the beach. _____

7 This is a person who is on holiday. _____

a tourist

a beach ball

a tsunami

an ice cream

2 Find the differences. Write sentences.

In Picture 2, the sandcastle is ...

Floods

1 Read this fact file about tsunamis and answer the question.

What happens after a tsunami? _____

A tsunami is a very big wave. It can happen when a lot of water moves suddenly. Underwater earthquakes often cause tsunamis because the ground at the bottom of the sea moves a lot. A tsunami wave can travel very quickly and very far. A tsunami can be 35 metres high, like a ten-floor building. It can move very fast, up to 970 km an hour. Tsunamis can kill people and animals and break down buildings. After a tsunami there are often floods, which cause more damage to the environment. We don't usually know when a tsunami will happen. Sometimes we know because the sea water moves a long way back from the beach.

2 Read the fact file again. Answer the questions.

1 What is a tsunami? <u>It's a very big wave.</u>

2 What can cause a tsunami? _____

3 What bad things can a tsunami do? _____

4 What can happen after a tsunami? _____

5 Do we know when tsunamis will happen? _____

3 Read the text about floods in the Student's Book again. Then read the text about tsunamis again. Match.

1 can sometimes help plants and animals

2 can travel very quickly

3 snow melts quickly

flood

tsunami

4 a river has too much water

5 can kill people and animals

6 can break down tall buildings

4 **Read the text. Tick ☑ the type of text it is.**

1 a blog about a flood ☐

2 a diary about a flood ☐

3 an advice sheet on floods ☐

Q:	How can I stay safe in a flood?
A:	Listen to the news for information about where you live. Do not walk in the streets when there is a flood. Stay with an adult. Do not swim or walk through the water. Switch off anything that works with electricity.
Q:	Who should I call?
A:	Call the emergency services. Listen carefully to what they say. If you need to leave your home, move quickly.
Q:	What should I do if I'm in a flood?
A:	First, don't panic! Try to float on your back or hold onto a big tree.
Q:	Can I drink tap water after a flood?
A:	No, you should boil the water first because it is dirty.

5 🛡 **Imagine there is a flood in your town. Complete the table with ideas from Activity 4.**

Do	Don't
stay with an adult	swim in the flood

6 🛡 **Write advice about flood safety. Use your ideas from Activity 5. Then draw.**

• Don't panic.
• _____
• _____
• _____

1 🎧 011 **Put the dialogue in order. Then listen and check.**

☐ **B:** When is it going to arrive?

☐ **A:** Good, so you're safe. Is there anyone in number 37?

☐ **B:** I'm calling from 39 Grange Road. The fire's at number 37.

1 **A:** Hello. How can we help you?

☐ **B:** Yes, I am.

☐ **A:** OK. Don't go in to check. Stay and wait for the fire engine.

☐ **B:** I'm calling to report a house fire next door to us.

☐ **A:** In about five minutes. Don't worry and keep a safe distance.

☐ **A:** Where are you calling from?

☐ **B:** I'm not sure.

☐ **A:** And are you outside the house?

2 **Look and write a dialogue. Use language from Activity 1.**

Woman: _Hello, how can we_
help you?

Boy: _____

_____

_____

_____

_____

_____

_____

_____

_____

_____

_____

What do I know?

1 Look and draw lines to make sentences.

1 We

	was	playing	cards	at 2 o'clock yesterday.
	are	watching	TV	at 5 o'clock yesterday.
	were	making	with toys	at 7 o'clock yesterday.

2 What

	was	you	did	in here this morning?
	is	your	do	in here tomorrow?
	were	yours	doing	in here next Tuesday?

3 Was

	she	flying	the piano	at 8 o'clock?
	they	doing	a kite	at 9 o'clock?
	he	playing	his homework	at 10 o'clock?

4 I

	was	watch	TV on	3 o'clock.
	were	watched	TV at	4 o'clock.
	am	watching	TV in	5 o'clock.

BIG QUESTION How can water be dangerous?

2 **Read and think. Then write two more.**

It can make floods. _____ _____

About me!

3 **Read. Then write about you and draw.**

I was reading a book yesterday
afternoon. I wasn't playing
computer games ...

_____
_____
_____
_____

4 Two return tickets

1 🛡 **Match and write the words.**

1 _____

3 _____

5 _____

plat ——— driver
ticket   of tea
train   lator
esca   case
a cup of   airs
a cup   form
ruck   tion
st   coffee
suit   sack
sta   office

2 **platform**

4 _____

6 _____

7 _____

8 _____

9 _____

10 _____

2 **Read and write words from Activity 1.**

1 This is a popular drink all over the world. You make it from beans.   **coffee**

2 Trains leave from and arrive at it.   _____

3 You carry your things in it. You carry it on your back.   _____

4 You walk up or down them.   _____

5 It takes you up or down.   _____

6 You buy your ticket there.   _____

3 🛡 **Imagine you are at a station. Where are you going? What can you see? What are you doing?**

I'm at the station. I'm going to _____

_____

_____

_____

1 Look and write *at*, *in* or *on*.

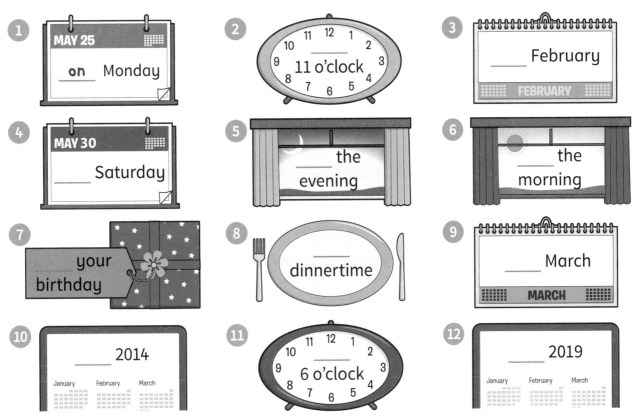

1 MAY 25 — **on** Monday

2 11 o'clock — _____

3 _____ February FEBRUARY

4 MAY 30 — _____ Saturday

5 _____ the evening

6 _____ the morning

7 _____ your birthday

8 _____ dinnertime

9 _____ March MARCH

10 _____ 2014 January February March

11 _____ 6 o'clock

12 _____ 2019 January February March

2 Circle the correct words.

1 He leaves for work **at / on** six o'clock **on / in** the morning.

2 We are having a party **in / on** Saturday **on / at** eight.

3 I'm going to visit my cousin **in / on** June.

4 The final volleyball match is **on / at** three o'clock **at / on** Saturday evening.

5 I go to bed **at / on** half past nine **in / on** winter.

6 We always watch TV **at / on** Sunday **at / in** the evening.

3 Write sentences about you.

When do you …

1 do your homework?

   I do my homework in the evening.

2 watch TV?

_____

3 go to bed?

_____

4 have lunch?

_____

5 relax?

_____

6 What month is your birthday?

_____

1 🛡 **Remember the song. Complete the sentences.**

1 The fantasy train is leaving _____at six_____ .

2 The drivers of the train are _____ .

3 Let's see a castle _____ .

4 We can see the town _____ .

5 Let's see the mountains _____ .

6 We can see the stars _____ .

2 🛡 **Complete the song with your ideas. Then draw a picture.**

The best way to travel is

The fantasy train.

It's leaving _____

From a platform in your brain.

A castle on _____

_____ in spring

_____ on _____

Let's go and see these things.

The mountains in _____

_____ far away

The stars in the evening

Let's see the world today.

1 **Complete the sentences with the correct form of the verbs.**

When the train arrived, …

1 I _____was eating_____ (eat) a sandwich.

2 John and Peter _____ (wait) on the platform.

3 a man _____ (read) a paper.

4 two men _____ (drink) tea.

5 a girl _____ (sit) on her suitcase.

6 a boy _____ (buy) a ticket.

2 **Write sentences. Use the words from the box.**

sit / garden   build / tree house   ride / bike   play / volleyball

When it started to rain, …

1 _they were playing volleyball_ . 2 _____.

3 _____ . 4 _____.

3 **Complete the sentences with the correct form of the verbs.**

1 Dad **was working** (work) in the garden when he _____hurt_____ (hurt) his hand.

2 I _____ (do) my homework when you _____ (phone) me.

3 When I _____ (leave) the party, my friends _____ (dance).

4 I _____ (listen) to music when Mum _____ (call) me.

1 Read the story *The tunnel* again. Then complete the sentences.

1 At Broom station, Lucy and Ben _see Horax and Zelda_ .

2 Ben tells Lucy to _____.

3 Zelda and Horax want to _____.

4 Ben can see that the train is _____.

5 When the conductor comes, Horax can't _____.

6 Horax and Zelda must _____.

2 What happened in the tunnel? Complete the story.

> couldn't find   took   ~~went~~   the tunnel   Horax's hat

When they _____ **went** _____ through _____,
Lucy _____ the tickets out of _____ and
Horax _____ them.

3 Read the story again. What can we learn from it? Draw 😃 or 😣.

( ) We do not need to be careful with our things.

( ) We should always be careful with our things.

1 🎧 012 **Listen and write the missing words. Then say with a friend.**

Anna: When are we going to wrap Dad's present?

James: Well, he's working in the garden at the moment – look.

Anna: Great! _____

_____ _____!

Hannah: Hey, Joe. What's that?

Joe: What? Where?

Hannah: That. Can't you see?

_____ _____

_____.

Joe: I can't see anything.

Hannah: Ah, it isn't there now.

Joe: Hey! My crisps!

2 **Look, read and write the words.**

chair   pear   stairs   wearing   hair   ~~bears~~

1 He's **scared** of the _____bears_____ .

2 **Clare** has got long _____.

3 Please **share** the _____.

4 **Where** are the _____?

5 He's _____ an old **pair** of trousers.

6 It's over **there** on that _____.

3 🎧 013 **Listen, say and check your answers.**

1 🎧 **014** **Listen and tick ☑ the box.**

1 Who was on the platform?

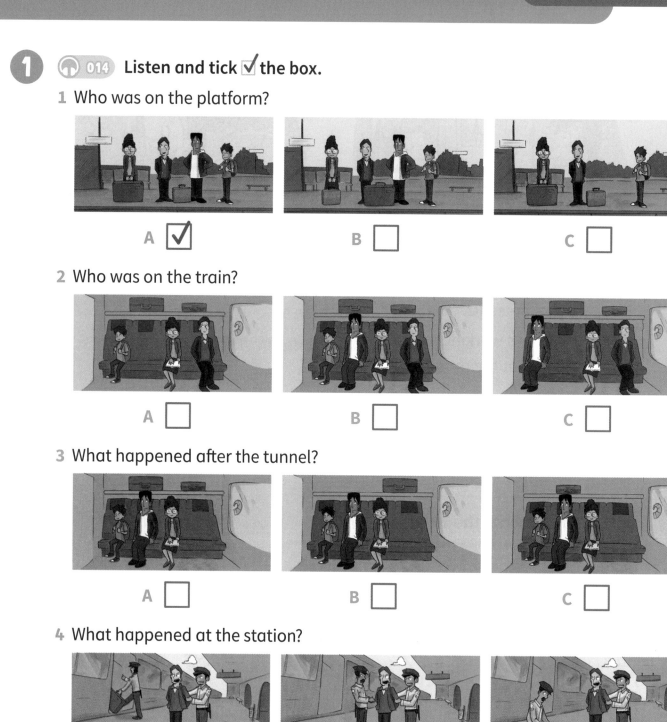

A ☑   B ☐   C ☐

2 Who was on the train?

A ☐   B ☐   C ☐

3 What happened after the tunnel?

A ☐   B ☐   C ☐

4 What happened at the station?

A ☐   B ☐   C ☐

5 What did the old lady do?

A ☐   B ☐   C ☐

1 **Read and choose the best answer.**

1 Bob: Did you buy a ticket to Bath?

  Ann: A It's seven pounds eighty.

  B Yes, I did.

  C It wasn't expensive.

2 Bob: How much is a single ticket to Bath?

  Ann: A It's five pounds twenty.

  B Here you are.

  C Thanks. Here's your ticket.

3 Bob: What time was your journey?

  Ann: A It was a long journey.

  B It was good.

  C It was at half past two.

4 Bob: When did you come home?

  Ann: A Not now.

  B In the evening.

  C Sometimes.

2 **Read the text. Choose the right words and write them on the lines.**

Example Stations are very busy and help people ___**travel**___ fast. Trains come

1 and go all through the day. Train drivers work early _____ the

2 morning or late _____ night. There is a noticeboard that tells you

3 what _____ the trains come and go. Today, the train to London

4 leaves at _____ six in the evening. The train from Oxford

5 arrives at _____ four in the afternoon.

Example	was travelling	travel	travelled
1	in	on	at
2	on	at	in
3	when	time	o'clock
4	half past	o'clock	quarter
5	o'clock	past	quarter past

Ways to travel

batteries

solar panels

1 **Read the text about different types of transport. Write *t* (true) or *f* (false).**

Electric trains use energy, but they can make energy too. When the train driver stops the train slowly, some parts of it produce electricity. This electricity can give energy to other trains going along the same line.

tank

Into the fut

cell buses

Fuel cell buses carry their power on top of them. The tanks on top of the bus have hydrogen. They take in oxygen from the air and make electricity. The electricity helps make the bus move. The bus is also very quiet, so there is no noise pollution either.

Solar powered buses have solar panels on the roof. The solar panels collect energy from the sun and store it in batteries. The buses use the batteries to move. The buses have extra batteries that store electricity for them to use at night.

1 All trains produce electricity. `f`

2 The electricity from the trains powers other trains. ☐

3 Fuel cell buses carry oxygen tanks. ☐

4 Fuel cell buses do not make a lot of noise. ☐

5 Solar buses use energy from the sun to move. ☐

6 At night, solar buses use batteries. ☐

2 🛡️ **Look at these different forms of transport. Tick ☑ the ones that are eco-friendly.**

 1 ☐

 2 ☐

 3 ☐

 4 ☐

 5 ☐

 6 ☐

3 **Read this text about Jim's invention. Complete the sentence.**

Jim's invention uses energy from the _____ and the _____ for the battery and to help the helicopter fly.

This is my eco-friendly helicopter.
It has solar panels on its propellers.
They collect sunlight from the sun.
The energy goes to the battery.
The battery helps the helicopter move.
At night, the fans collect energy from the wind and help the helicopter fly.
It isn't very fast, but it is quiet.

4 🛡️ **Invent an eco-friendly form of transport. Write about it, then draw a picture.**

My form of transport is _____

_____

_____

_____

_____

_____

1 🎧 015 **Put the dialogue in order. Then listen and check.**

☐ **A:** To London. OK. When do you want to leave?

☐ **B:** Here you are.

☐ **A:** Single or return?

☐ **B:** Half past eight is fine. How much is the ticket?

[1] **A:** Hello. How can I help you?

☐ **B:** Thank you. Oh, and what platform number is it, please?

☐ **A:** The return ticket is £42.

☐ **B:** Return, please.

☐ **A:** Thanks. And here's your change.

☐ **B:** I want to go to London, please.

☐ **A:** Platform 2.

☐ **B:** In the morning.

☐ **A:** There's a train at seven and one at half past eight.

2 **Look and write a dialogue. Use language from Activity 1.**

Man: _Hello. Can I help you?_

Boy: _____

_____

_____

_____

_____

_____

_____

_____

_____

_____

Cambridge
Single
???

£15.20
platform 3

What do I know?

1 Colour the bricks to make sentences. Write in the missing words.

1	When the train	_____ TV when	Saturday.
2	My birthday party	arrived, Dad was	you phoned me.
3	I was	holiday _____	August for two weeks.
4	We're going on	too fast	when he _____ an accident.
5	Bob was driving	is _____	buying a cup of coffee.

2 🛡 **Read and think. Then write three more.**

BIG QUESTION What's the best way to travel?

The best way to travel is by bicycle, _____,
_____ and _____.

About me!

3 🛡 **Read. Then write about you and draw.**

Yesterday, I was walking to school _____
when I saw an electric car. It was ... _____
_____ _____
_____ _____

5 Police!

1 Look, read and number the sentences.

a ☐ He's got long dark hair. It's straight.

b ☐ He's got fair curly hair. He's got a beard and a moustache.

c ☐ He's got short blond hair. He's got a scar below his mouth.

2 Read and draw Danni's face.

3 Write and draw a *Wanted* poster.

★
WANTED
Dangerous Danni

She's got long hair. It's black. She's got a long scar on her face and a small scar between her eyes. She's very dangerous.

DON'T speak to her. Call the police!

★
WANTED

1 Look at the pictures. Read and write *t* (true) or *f* (false).

2001   Now

1 Dad used to have long hair. | t |
2 Dad used to have a scar. | |
3 Dad used to have a beard. | |
4 Dad used to have a moustache. | |
5 Dad used to have straight hair. | |
6 Dad used to have dark hair. | |

2 Complete the sentences. Use the words from the box.

cry   sleep   eat   ~~drink~~   play   crawl

When I was a baby, …

1 I ___used to drink___ milk.

2 I _____ a lot.

3 I _____ in a cot.

4 I _____ baby food.

5 I _____ on my hands and knees.

6 I _____ with my teddy bear.

3 Write sentences about you.

When I was four, …

1 _____

2 _____

3 _____

1 Remember the song. What did Dad use to look like? Tick ✓ the correct pictures.

1
a □
b □
c □

2
a □
b □
c □

3
a □
b □
c □

2 Draw your mum or dad. What did they use to look like?
What do they look like now?

Then

Now

3 Complete the sentences about your mum or dad.

Mum / Dad used to _____

_____

Now Mum / Dad has _____

_____

1 Read and write the words.

> wear   help   ~~arrive~~   do   learn

When I was a schoolboy, …

1 I had to ____arrive____ at school before 7 o'clock.

2 I had to _____ a uniform.

3 I had to _____ French, German and Spanish.

4 I had to _____ homework for two hours every night.

5 I had to _____ the teacher with the younger students.

2 Look and write sentences.

When I lived at home, I had to work hard every day.

1 __I had to tidy up.__

2 _____

3 _____

4 _____

5 _____

6 _____

Now I live in my own house, I don't have to do things every day!

3 Imagine you are 25 years old. Write sentences about what you had to do when you were young.

1 __When I was young, I had to__ _____.

2 _____

3 _____

1 🛡 **Read the story *The Mysterious H* again. Complete the text.**

There used to be a thief called the Mysterious H. He used to steal necklaces, bracelets and watches from **(1)** __jewellers__ in London. He also used to steal famous paintings and **(2)** _____ of art from museums all over the **(3)** _____. One day he stole the Queen's **(4)** _____. The story of the Mysterious H was in all the **(5)** _____. He even stole the top of the Eiffel Tower! Grandpa knew it was always the same man because he always used to leave a **(6)** _____ with an H on it. Grandpa never caught him.

2 **Tick ☑ the correct sentences.**

1 Grandpa and the Mysterious H used to be friends. ☐

2 No jewellery shop in London was safe. ☑

3 Museums gave the Mysterious H works of art. ☐

4 Grandpa tried to find the Mysterious H. ☐

5 The waiter and the Mysterious H have something with the same letter. ☐

3 **Where did the Mysterious H steal these things from? Draw lines and write sentences.**

a museum
a castle
a jeweller's shop
an art gallery
Paris

1 __He stole the painting from an art gallery.__

2 _____

3 _____

4 _____

5 _____

1 🎧 016 **Listen and write the missing words. Then say with a friend.**

1

Abby: You're famous.

Chris: I'm sorry, what did you say?

Abby: You're famous. Look.
You're _____
_____ _____
_____.

Chris: Oh no! I must change my
hair again.

2

Jeremy: Oh no! It got away!

Lionel: Again? You're just not lucky
today!

Jeremy: _____ _____
_____ _____.

Lionel: Maybe next time.

2 **Look, read and number the sentences.**

1  **2**  **3**  **4**

a ☐ They were **wa**l**k**ing in **N**o**r**th **P**a**r**k when a terrible **st**o**r**m **st**a**r**ted.

b [1] **P**au**l** and **D**a**w**n went out at qu**ar**ter past **f**ou**r** in the **m**o**r**ning.

c ☐ The rescue team **s**aw the light and took **P**au**l** and **D**a**w**n to their car.

d ☐ They couldn't find their **car** in the **d**a**r**k, so **D**a**w**n used her **t**o**r**ch.

3 🎧 017 **Listen, say and check your answers.**

1 🛡️ **Read the story *The Gentleman Robber* again. Correct the sentences.**

1 One day, a tall man with long dark hair walked into a museum shop.

   One day, a tall man with short blond hair walked into a jeweller's shop.

2 He asked to see the cheapest watch and he bought it.

_____

3 The thief bought a necklace from another jeweller.

_____

4 They called him the Gentleman Robber because he always said, 'Thank you'.

_____

5 The artist drew a picture of a doctor.

_____

6 The Gentleman Robber made a mistake, then the police returned a stolen watch.

_____

7 The Gentleman Robber stole again and the police caught him.

_____

2 **Read the story again. How did the Gentleman Robber mend his ways? Tick ☑ the correct sentence.**

1 He took the doctor out of prison. ☐

2 He returned a stolen item so the police could let out the doctor. ☐

3 He told the jeweller who he was. ☐

3 🖐️ 🛡️ **Read the story again and think. Draw 😃 or 😖.**

○ You should always try to correct your mistakes.

○ You shouldn't care about the mistakes you made in the past.

1 **Look at the pictures. Answer the questions and then write the whole story.**

Complete the sentences about pictures 1 and 2.

1 Where is the boy? _____

2 The boy takes some _____ and puts them in his _____.

Answer the questions about pictures 3 and 4.

3 Does the shop owner catch the boy? _____

4 Who does he call? _____

Now write two sentences about pictures 5 and 6. Then write the whole story.

5 _____

6 _____

Sketches

1 **Look at these drawings. They are all sketches. Are the sentences about sketches *t* (true) or *f* (false)?**

1 Sketches are always in black and white. ☐

2 Sketches are always of people. ☐

portrait

pochade

croquis

2 **Read this text about sketches. Complete with the words from Activity 1.**

A sketch is usually a black and white drawing. Sometimes a sketch is in colour. In ancient Egypt, artists used to sketch on a kind of paper called papyrus. Later, art students made sketches first, then they painted a bigger picture. Sketches became a popular thing to do. People drew sketches of places, animals and other things. In the past, there weren't any photos, so sketches were important. People could look at them and remember things. There are three different types of sketches:

1 _____
These sketches show people, often just their faces. The artists use light and dark lines with lots of shading.

2 _____
These sketches often show a person's body. People who make clothes, draw these kinds of sketches. Artists usually use light, curved lines.

3 _____
These are small sketches of places. They are usually in colour. The artist makes them quickly before they make the finished painting.

3 🛡 Look at these two sketches of people. What techniques and materials do they use? Write the words under each sketch. One word can go under both sketches.

colour   ~~charcoal~~   shading   pen   thick lines   thin lines   curved lines

charcoal _____   _____

_____   _____   _____   _____

_____   _____

4 🛡 Sketch an object in your home that you like, or a person. What technique and materials did you use?

For my sketch, I used _____

_____

_____

_____

_____

_____

_____

_____

_____

_____

_____

1 Match the questions and answers.

1 Where do you like to read?

2 How many books do you read a week?

3 What are your favourite kind of books?

4 Do you like funny stories?

5 What other kind of things do you read?

6 What's best, watching TV or reading?

a Reading, definitely, but I like TV.

b I love crime stories.

c The best place is in bed!

d About two.

e No, I don't. I never read them.

f I read comics and I sometimes read my dad's newspaper.

2 Look at Activity 1. <u>Underline</u> the mistakes. Then write the correct sentences.

Lucy <u>likes reading, but she loves watching TV</u> too. Her favourite place to read is on the sofa. She reads more than three books a week. Her favourite kind of books are science fiction stories. She never reads historical novels. As well as reading books, she reads comics and magazines.

<u>Lucy loves reading, but she likes watching TV too.</u>

_____

_____

_____

_____

_____

3 Write about your reading habits.

I like reading in bed.

What do I know?

1 Look and draw lines to make sentences.

1

Mum's family

used to	living	in France	in the 1980s.
used	lived	by France	at the 1980s.
use to	live	on France	on the 1980s.

2

I

had	tidying	my bedroom	yesterday.
have to	tidied	the kitchen	Monday.
has to	tidy	the living room	today.

3

My dad

had	help	my dad	in the shop.
had to	helped	his dad	in the cinema.
have to	helping	our dad	at the zoo.

BIG QUESTION How can we describe people?

2 Read and think. Then write three more.

We can use the words: short hair, curly hair, _____,
_____ and _____ .

About me!

3 Read. Then write about you and draw.

I used to have short curly hair. _____
It was dark. I used to play all day, _____
but I had to go to bed early. _____

6 Mythical beasts

1 Look and complete the words.

1 h o r n

2 _ o _ g _ _ _

3 _ _ c _

4 _ _ a t _ _ _ s

5 _ _ _ _ g

6 _ _ _ c _

7 t _ _ _ _

8 _ _ a _ _ s

2 Look, read and number the texts.

1

a ☐ This dragon has got wings. The feathers on them are beautiful. They've got orange and yellow patterns. The dragon's neck is long and it's got scales. There are also scales on its back and there are feathers on its back too. It's got a short tail, a long tongue and two horns.

2

b ☐ This dragon has got wings. The yellow feathers on the wings are beautiful. The dragon has got scales on its back and also on its long neck. It's got a long tongue, a horn and a short tail.

3 Draw a dragon. What does it look like? Write.

This dragon has got _____

_____

_____

_____

1 Read and write *t* (true) or *f* (false).

FACT FILE

1 **The world's longest snake**

The python holds the world record for the longest snake. It's longer than the anaconda, but anacondas are the world's fattest snakes.

python

anaconda

2 **The most aggressive animal**

Hippos are very aggressive. They aren't scared of humans and are much more dangerous than lions.

3 **The world's worst singer?**

The 'crex-crex' song of the corncrake sounds so terrible that this bird is certainly the world's worst singer.

4 **Crocodiles – the smallest and the heaviest**

The smallest crocodile is the dwarf crocodile of West Africa. It's 1.5 m long. The heaviest crocodiles are saltwater crocodiles, which can grow to 7 m long and weigh over 1,000 kg!

1 Anacondas are fatter than pythons. `t`

2 The longest snake is the anaconda. ☐

3 Hippos are very dangerous, but they run from humans. ☐

4 The song of the corncrake is not very nice at all. ☐

5 Saltwater crocodiles aren't longer than dwarf crocodiles. ☐

2 Write sentences.

1 Anacondas / fat / snakes in the world.

   Anacondas are the fattest snakes in the world.

2 Hippos / dangerous / lions.

   _____

3 Corncrakes / bad / singers in the animal kingdom.

   _____

4 Dwarf crocodiles / small / saltwater crocodiles.

   _____

1 🛡 **Remember the song. Complete the sentences.**

biggest   best   jump   scales   feathers   ~~longest~~   scariest   fin

1 The Titanoboa was the ___longest___ snake. It had _____ .

2 The dinosaur book is the _____ book. The animals _____
out when you open it.

3 The Megalodon was the _____ shark. It had a giant _____ .

4 The Gastornis was the _____ bird. It had very big _____ .

2 **Look at these animals from the past. Read and circle the correct words.**

beak

dodo

tusks

woolly mammoth

Pyrenean ibex

1 The Pyrenean ibex had long **wings** / (**horns**) but short hair. It was the **good** /
best mountain climber.

2 The dodo was a big bird. It had **long** / **short** wings. It had a **big** / **small** beak.

3 The woolly mammoth was the **biggest** / **smallest** animal on land. It had long
brown fur. It had the **longest** / **shortest** tusks.

3 🛡 **Choose an animal from Activity 2. Write a verse about it.**

The _____ was a very _____ .

It's the _____ in my book,

With _____ and _____ .

Please come and have a look.

1 Write questions for the answers. Use the words from the box.

Pegasus   the Sphinx   a mermaid   a unicorn   the Phoenix   ~~a centaur~~

1 _What does a centaur look like?_   It's half horse and half man.

2 _____ She's got the head of a woman and the tail of a fish.

3 _____ It's a bird with very big wings and red and golden feathers.

4 _____ It looks like a horse, but it's got wings and can fly.

5 _____ It's a white horse with a long horn in the middle of its head.

6 _____ It looks like a lion with a human head.

2 Read the dialogue. Write *1, 2, 3* or *4*.

A: What does Cloud _____ look like?

B: I think it looks like a dog. It's driving a car.

Write dialogues about the other pictures.

A: _____

B: _____

A: _____

B: _____

A: _____

B: _____

1 Read the story *The secret door* again. Then put the sentences in order.

☐ The children find a way out, but they have to jump into the pool.

[1] Lucy finds a little door in the dragon.

☐ Horax and Zelda see Ben and Lucy, but the children run away.

☐ On the side of the pool, they find the next line for the rhyme.

☐ The children open it and go in.

☐ It's a trap! Horax closes the door and they can't get out.

2 Complete Horax's diary entry.

Today was a (1) _____**bad**_____ day for Zelda and me. We saw
(2) _____.

They were looking at (3) _____. We were
sure the next line (4) _____,
but then they opened (5) _____ and
(6) _____. Zelda and I
(7) _____.

In the end, the children (8) _____ and they
(9) _____. Zelda and I were very
(10) _____.

3 Read the story again and think. Colour the circles green for *yes* and red for *no*.

◯ You should think about your safety before doing anything.

◯ It's OK to do things without thinking about your safety first.

1 🎧 018 **Listen and write the missing words. Then say with a friend.**

Ollie: I don't believe it. The ball's really high up in the tree.

Jem: And that tree's too dangerous to climb.

Ollie: We could get my dad's ladder.

Jem: Yes. That's _____ _____ _____.

Mum: Where are you?

Dad: He's here somewhere.

Connor: Hee, hee, hee.

Mum: _____ _____ _____ _____ _____!

Connor: Hee, hee, hee.

Mum and Dad: There you are!

Connor: Ha!

2 **Complete the table with the words from the box.**

~~weather~~   eat   team   feather   beans   bread   head   meat

beast

_____
_____
_____

treasure

weather
_____
_____
_____

3 🎧 019 **Listen, say and check your answers.**

1 Read the story. Choose a word from the box. Write the correct word next to numbers 1–5. There is one example.

Penny loves reading about different _____animals_____ .

Last week, Penny and her friends did a project on animals from the past or present. She found all the information on a website. She chose a **(1)** _____ that had big wings and horns. 'I think dinosaurs were the **(2)** _____ animals in the world. They were very scary too,' she said to her class.

Her friend Ben did a project on animals in the wild. 'My project is about eagles. They have strong **(3)** _____ and beautiful long feathers.'

Anne didn't know what animal to choose. 'How about goldfish?' said Penny. 'They have **(4)** _____ and long fins. They can also be **(5)** _____.'

'That's a great idea,' said Anne.

animals	wings	pets
plants	strongest	scales
horn	dinosaur	smallest

2 Now choose the best name for the story. Tick ✓ one box.

Penny's animal book ☐

A lesson about animals ☐

Animal projects ☐

1 **Look and read. Choose the correct words and write them on the lines.
There is one example.**

necklace

neck

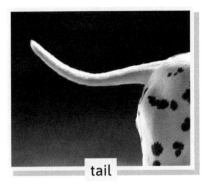
tail

stairs

escalator

island

village

bracelet

Example

We walk up and down them to get to different floors of a place.   _stairs_

Questions

1 A place smaller than a city or town in the countryside.   _____

2 You wear this on the end of your arm.   _____

3 It's usually long and many animals have this on their backs.   _____

4 This joins the head and body.   _____

5 It's a piece of land with water all around it.   _____

Dinosaurs

1 Read about three other animals from long ago. Tick ☑ the correct sentence.

1 They lived at the same time as dinosaurs. ☐

2 They disappeared when a big object hit the Earth. ☐

A long time ago, a big object from space hit Earth. All the dinosaurs and plants died, but some other kinds of animals didn't die.

These green sea turtles lived more than 200 million years ago. They are very clever animals. When it is too hot or dry, they go under the ground. They wait there for cool weather. These animals are the largest turtles in the world.

The platypus lived at the same time as green sea turtles. They used to be much longer than platypuses today. They lay eggs, but they also give their babies milk. They only live in Australia, in small rivers or lakes.

Bees didn't live in water, but they lived at the same time as the dinosaurs. They appeared when the first flowers and plants appeared. This was 145 million years ago. Some people think they disappeared when the dinosaurs disappeared, but then came back later. But we don't know if this is true.

2 Read the text again and match.

1 The dinosaurs and plants died   a when it wants to be cool.

2 The green sea turtle is   b bees disappeared with the dinosaurs.

3 The green sea turtle goes underground

4 Platypuses today are   c in water.

5 The platypus lives   d smaller than platypuses in the past.

6 People don't know if   e because a big object hit Earth.

    f larger than other turtles.

6

3 🛡 Read and write *herbivore*, *carnivore* or *omnivore*.

1 Green iguanas only eat plants. They have sharp teeth, so they can eat thick plants. They didn't live during the dinosaur period.

　herbivore

2 Crocodiles are more than 240 million years old. They only eat meat and have very long and sharp teeth.

_____

3 Catfish live in the sea. They eat plants and other small fish. They are about 15 million years old.

_____

4 Elephants are more than 55 million years old. They eat grass, small plants, fruit and roots. They use their long trunks to get food from tall trees.

_____

5 Snakes have been on our planet for more than 102 million years. They eat mice, fish, frogs and lizards.

_____

6 Zebras eat grass, herbs, leaves, flowers and twigs. They have long necks and eat a lot. They are only 4 million years old.

_____

4 🛡 Find an animal that you think is interesting. What does it look like? Where does it live? What does it eat? Write, then draw a picture.

_____

_____

_____

_____

_____

_____

1 🎧 020 **Put the dialogue in order. Then listen and check.**

☐ **B:** What's strange about a white horse?

☐ **A:** In the garden behind our house, 23 Queen's Park. It's eating all the flowers.

☐ **B:** Really? What does it look like?

1 **A:** Good afternoon. Can I speak to the director of the zoo, please?

☐ **B:** OK. Try not to scare it. I'm coming to your house right now.

☐ **A:** Well, it looks like a horse – a white horse.

☐ **B:** That's me. How can I help you?

☐ **A:** It's got a horn.

☐ **B:** A white horse with a horn. Then it's a unicorn. Where did you find it?

☐ **A:** I've got a strange animal. I found it this afternoon.

2 **Look and write a dialogue. Use language from Activity 1.**

Girl: I've got a strange animal. I found it this afternoon.

Boy: _____

_____

_____

_____

_____

_____

_____

What do I know?

1 Colour the bricks to make sentences. Write in the missing words.

1	What does	best sister _____	_____?
2	You're the	your sister	my mum.
3	What do	mermaids look	_____ the world!
4	That's the ugliest	is taller _____	the world!
5	My aunt	dog	look _____ like?

BIG QUESTION What were animals like long ago?

  2 Read and think. Then write two more.

They had scales and long tails. _____

_____

_____

About me!

3 Read. Then write about you and draw.

My favourite animal is the parrot. _____

It has colourful feathers and strong _____

wings. It's an omnivore. _____

7 Orchestra practice

1 Complete the crossword.

¹ t a m b o u r i n e

Across

1.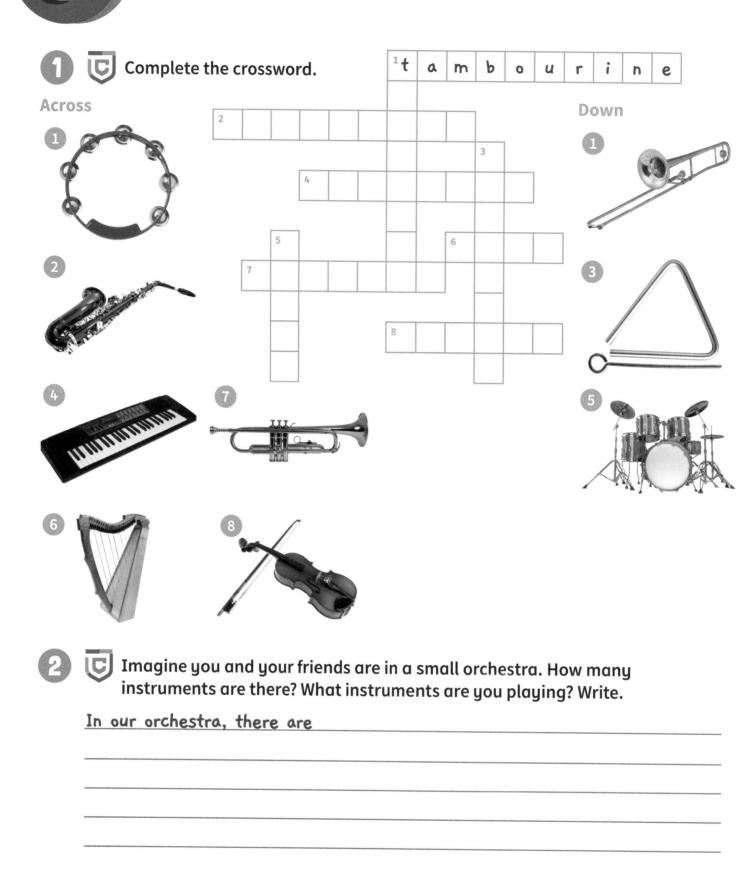

2.

4.

6.

Down

1.

3.

5.

7.

8.

2 Imagine you and your friends are in a small orchestra. How many instruments are there? What instruments are you playing? Write.

In our orchestra, there are _____

_____

_____

_____

_____

1 Read and write the words.

hers   theirs   his   yours   ~~mine~~   ours

1 Is this your bike, Ken?

Yes, it's _____mine_____.

2 Is this Peter's guitar?

Yes, it's _____.

3 Is this my pen?

Yes, it's _____.

4 That's a nice scooter. Is it Jane's?

Yes, it's _____.

5 Is this where you and Lily live?

Yes, this house is _____.

6 This is Peter and Tom's car.

Is it really _____?

2 Change the sentences.

1 It's my dog.   It's _____mine_____.

2 It's Mia's cat.   It's _____.

3 They are John and Lucy's horses.   They're _____.

4 This house is Ruby's and mine.   It's _____.

5 It's John's violin.   It's _____.

6 It's not my cap. It's your cap.   It's _____.

3 Look and write sentences.

It's mine

_____

_____

_____

_____

1 🛡 **Remember the song. Tick ✓ or cross ✗. Write the correct sentences.**

1 Kate plays the harp. ✗ Kate plays the keyboard.

2 Hope plays the keyboard. ☐ _____

3 Tim plays the trumpet. ☐ _____

4 Dave plays the drums. ☐ _____

5 Tim plays Hope's trumpet. ☐ _____

2 **Follow the lines. Answer the questions.**

Roy   Sally   Anne   Lee   Pedro

1 Roy doesn't play the keyboard. He plays the _____ trombone _____.

2 Sally plays the _____.

3 Anne doesn't play the trumpet. She plays the _____.

4 Lee plays the _____.

5 Pedro doesn't play the trombone. He plays the _____.

3 **Write about the people in the Activity 2.**

1 The trombone is Roy's. It's his.

2 _____

3 _____

4 _____

5 _____

1 Read and circle.

1 Matt is the boy (who) / **which** plays the guitar.

2 Mexico is the country **which** / **where** my cousins live.

3 The house **who** / **which** you can see over there is Bob's.

4 Claire is the girl **where** / **who** is a very good footballer.

5 The instrument **which** / **who** George plays is the saxophone.

6 London is the city **who** / **where** I'd like to live.

2 Read and write *who*, *which* or *where*.

1 Max is the boy _____who_____ reads lots of books.

2 The instrument _____ my friend plays is the violin.

3 The town _____ my grandparents live is near the coast.

4 Maria is the girl _____ likes listening to music.

5 The pen _____ is on the floor is Will's.

6 The farm _____ we ride horses is in the mountains.

3 Look and write four more sentences with *who* or *which*.

The boy who is reading is Jack.

The saxophone which is next to the sofa is Jack's.

_____

_____

_____

_____

1 🛡 Remember the story *At the concert hall*. Read and write the words.

apple   hides   banana   ~~café~~   takes   cup   line   open   starts   to

Lucy and Ben go to the **(1)** _____café_____ for a drink. They order orange juice, an **(2)** _____, hot chocolate and a **(3)** _____. Then Ben sees the **(4)** _____ on Lucy's **(5)** _____. When the children are having their drinks, Horax looks in Ben's rucksack and he **(6)** _____ out the map. The conductor sees Horax and wants him **(7)** _____ leave. Horax **(8)** _____ the map in the trumpet. When Ben and Lucy come back, they see that Ben's rucksack is **(9)** _____. When the trumpet player **(10)** _____, the children find the map.

2 🛡 Read and write *t* (true) or *f* (false).

1 Pictures 1 and 2: The children know that the line is in the café. [f]

2 Picture 4: Lucy can't read the line. [ ]

3 Picture 5: When Horax says, 'Very nice of you, kids. Thank you,' he is talking to Ben and Lucy. [ ]

4 Picture 6: When the conductor arrives, Horax thinks of a trick. [ ]

5 Picture 7: The children know the map is in the trumpet. [ ]

6 Picture 8: The trick which Horax plays doesn't work. [ ]

3 Look and answer the questions.

1 Is this Ben's?

No, it isn't his.

It's the conductor's.

2 Is this Lucy's?

_____

_____

3 Is this Horax's?

_____

_____

4 Is this the conductor's?

_____

_____

1 🎧 021 **Listen and write the missing words. Then say with a friend.**

Mum: Be careful with those plates, Tom. Maybe you should only take two at a time?

Tom: Don't worry, Mum ... Whoops!

Mum: Tom!

Tom: _____ _____ _____, Mum. I really am.

Debs: Where's Frank?

George: I don't know. There are just too many people.

Debs: Hey, look. There he is. Over there. Frank! Frank!

George: Oh yes, there he is! _____ _____, Debs!

2 **Write the words from the box in the _shi<u>r</u>t_ or the _d<u>oo</u>r_.**

~~world~~ floor bird work call thirsty orchestra keyboard
horn curly sword her four first purple talk

world

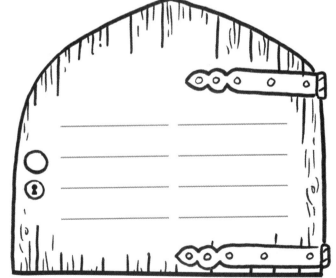

3 🎧 022 **Listen, say and check your answers.**

1 Read Tristan's story again. Match the sentences.

1 The orchestra players were excited because

2 The players had five days to

3 The trumpet player said people

4 The violin player said people

5 The trombonist said

6 The triangle player

7 At the concert, there were many

8 Tristan's note was

a learn the new music.

b people in the audience.

c the conductor had new music for them.

d feel happy when they hear his music.

e had one note to play.

f the most important in the music.

g feel relaxed when they hear her music.

h people dance when they hear his music.

2 Complete the summary with the words from the box.

important   ~~conductor~~   instrument   musicians   notes   orchestra   player

On Monday morning, the **(1)** __conductor__ had some new music for his orchestra. The players looked at the music to see how many **(2)** _____ they had to play.

Tristan, who was the triangle **(3)** _____, was quiet and sad because he only had one note to play. All the other musicians wanted to be the most important **(4)** _____ in the orchestra. On Friday evening, hundreds of people came to hear the **(5)** _____. All the musicians played loudly, but Tristan just sat and watched all the other **(6)** _____. Then, the hall was silent. No trumpets, no drums, no violins, no trombone.

'Ting!' Everyone in the hall heard Tristan's note. They all stood up from their chairs and started cheering. The conductor walked past the trumpet players, the trombonists, the drummers and the violin players. He thanked Tristan for playing the most **(7)** _____ note.

3 Read the story again and think. Draw 😃 or 😣.

◯ All team members are important.

◯ Team members with lots of work are the most important.

1 **Read the text. Choose the right words and write them on the lines.**

THE VIOLIN

The violin is the **(1)** _smallest_ member
of the string family. It is sometimes called a fiddle. A big orchestra **(2)** _____
more violins than any other single instrument. The violin section has two areas, the first
and second violins. The first violins play the highest notes, and the second violins play
the lower notes. A person **(3)** _____ plays the violin is called a violinist. It is one
of the most important orchestral instruments. In the past, some composers wrote music
only for the violin.

Almost 70 pieces of wood make a violin **(4)** _____ most of its parts are glued
together with a special glue.

The modern violin **(5)** _____ about 400 years old. But other string
instruments that look **(6)** _____ the violin are more than 1,000 years old.
Violins come in different sizes. There are eight main sizes, from 23cm to 36cm.

1	smallest	smaller	small
2	have	has	had
3	which	he	who
4	but	because	and
5	is	was	are
6	as	like	to

Instrument FAMILIES

1 Look at these instruments.
How do you play them? Write the words.

pluck   blow   hit   shake

xylophone
hit

bagpipes

lute

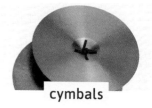
cymbals

harmonica

santoor

maracas

cabasa

2 Write the instruments in Activity 1 in the correct place. Some can go in more than one place.

string

wind

percussion
xylophone,

3 Look at this instrument. Read the text and answer the questions.

The fotoplayer

The first films were not colour and they had no sound. They were silent films. A person used to play the fotoplayer next to the stage when the film was playing. A fotoplayer had a piano, drums and percussion. It could also make lots of different sound effects for the film, such as bells, horns and the sound of horses' feet. Can you see the different instruments?

1 What different instruments were in the fotoplayer?

2 What was a fotoplayer used for?

4 **Read about an unusual orchestra. Tick ✓ the correct sentences.**

carrot flute

pumpkin drum

cucumber trumpet

pepper horn

Carrots, cucumbers and pumpkins. These are some things the Vienna vegetable orchestra uses to make music. Pumpkins become drums and carrots make very good flutes, recorders and xylophones. When you move two leeks together, they sound loud and high, like a violin. When you move the outside of two onions together, they sound like maracas. Cucumbers and carrots make fantastic trumpets. If you add a pepper, they make a very loud noise. Peppers also make great horns.

The players take out the insides of the vegetables to make the instruments. They make soup with the inside of the vegetables. They give the soup to people after the show. The players also give them the vegetable instruments as a present.

1 The orchestra makes carrots with flutes. ☐

2 They make drums with pumpkins. ☑

3 Leeks sound like a violin. ☐

4 Maracas make onion soup. ☐

5 A pepper on a carrot makes a loud noise. ☐

6 The orchestra eat soup before they play a show. ☐

5 **Find different vegetables in your fridge. What instruments can you make with them? Write and then draw.**

There's a carrot. I can make a flute.

1 Match the questions and answers.

1 Do you play an instrument, Lily?
2 Would you like to play an instrument?
3 Who's your favourite singer?
4 Justin Bieber? Is he from the USA?
5 And what's your favourite song?
6 Is there a song which you really don't like?

a It's Justin Bieber.
b My favourite song? It's probably 'Never say never'.
c Yes, I'd like to play the violin.
d No, not by Justin! But I really don't like 'Someone like you' by Adele.
e No, I don't.
f No, he's from Canada.

2 Look at Activity 1. <u>Underline</u> the mistakes. Then write the correct sentences.

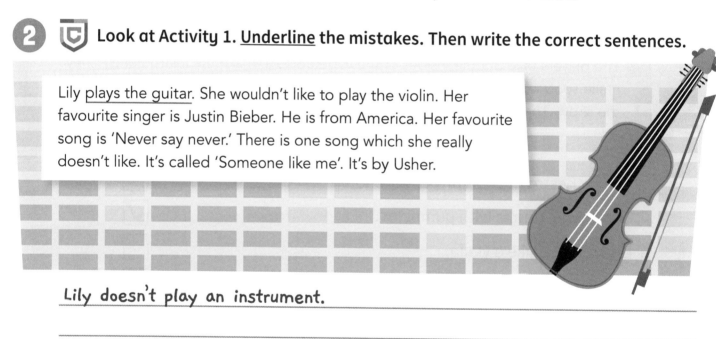

Lily <u>plays the guitar</u>. She wouldn't like to play the violin. Her favourite singer is Justin Bieber. He is from America. Her favourite song is 'Never say never.' There is one song which she really doesn't like. It's called 'Someone like me'. It's by Usher.

Lily doesn't play an instrument.

_____

_____

_____

_____

3 Write about yourself and music.

I play the piano and I'd like to play ...

What do I know?

1 Look and draw lines to make sentences.

1 It

isn't you	cap.	They're	my.
isn't your	caps.	He's	me.
isn't yours	book.	It's	mine.

2 The recorders

which	are on	the sofa	are us.
who	are next to	the chair	are ours.
where	are under	the cupboard	are violins.

3 I

thinks	this ball	were	hers.
think	these balls	are	yours.
thinking	those balls	is	theirs.

4 The girl

who is	sitting	opposite the tree	is my sister.
where is	sits	next to the tree	is hers.
which is	sit	on the tree	is my brother.

2  Read and think.
Then write two more.

BIG QUESTION How are musical instruments different?

You can hit some instruments. _____

_____

 About me!

3 Read. Then write about you and draw.

My favourite instrument is the piano.
It has keys and strings. It's a
percussion and string instrument.

_____

_____

_____

8 In the planetarium

1 **Match the definitions and answers.**

1 This is something which you use to look at the night sky.

2 He or she flies in a rocket.

3 Earth is one of these.

4 This has got a tail and it flies through the sky.

5 People stay and work here in space.

6 The night sky is full of these.

7 You use this to fly to the moon.

8 This is an alien spaceship.

9 The planet Earth has one of these.

a planet

b rocket

c UFO

d stars

e comet

f telescope

g astronaut

h moon

i space station

2 **Look at Activity 1. Number the pictures.**

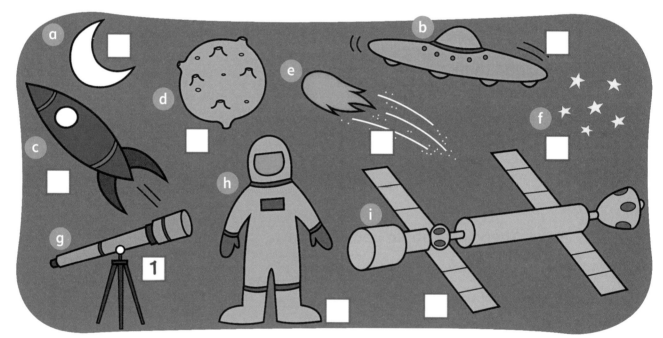

3 Imagine you are looking through a telescope. What can you see? What does it look like?

I can see _____

_____.

1 Follow the lines. Write the names and the sentences.

 Ana
 Kyle
 Elena
 Adam
 Lucia

Adam _____ : __I'll be a__ n u rs _e_ .
_____ : _____ _ str _ n ___ t.
_____ : _____ f _ r _ f _ ght _ _ r.
_____ : _____ c _ n d _ _ ct _ r.
_____ : _____ p _ _ l _ c _ _ _ ff _ c _ r.

2 🛡 Write five sentences about you.

When I grow up, I'll be an explorer. _____

I'll look for treasure. _____

I'll have lots of fun. _____

I'll travel the world. _____

I'll be very happy. _____

1 🛡 **Remember the song. Correct the sentences.**

1 The astronaut will build a space station. *No, she'll live in a space station.*

2 She'll stand on the rocket. _____

3 She'll fly to the sun in the rocket. _____

4 She'll ride on a comet and paint its tail. _____

5 She'll fly slowly in outer space. _____

6 She'll visit some of the stars. _____

2 **What will you do when you're an astronaut? Write sentences.
Then write one more and draw.**

~~fly~~ look take

1 *I'll fly to the moon.*

2 _____

3 _____

4 _____

3 🛡 **Imagine you visit Jupiter. What will you do? Write four sentences.**

I'll collect some rocks.

1 **Write the adverbs to complete the sentences.**

1 John is a good footballer, but yesterday he played ___**badly**___ (bad).

2 She sang the song _____ (beautiful) at the concert.

3 Uncle Rob is too fast on the road. He drives _____ (dangerous).

4 When he saw the big dog, he ran back to his car _____ (quick).

5 She loved her new toy and played _____ (happy) with it all day.

6 He didn't want to wake his brother, so he spoke very _____ (quiet).

2 **Write sentences. Make adverbs with the adjectives from the box.**

bad ~~careful~~ quiet loud

1 He _'s working carefully._

2 They _____.

3 She _____.

4 He _____.

3 **Write four sentences about you. Use adverbs.**

I ride my bike carefully.

_____

_____

_____

_____

1 Read the story *The trap* again. Then put the sentences in order.

☐ Zelda finds a poem.

☐ Lucy and Ben close the door.

☐ Ben's grandfather and a police officer arrive.

1 Lucy and Ben can't find the clue anywhere and they go for a drink.

☐ The police officer takes Horax and Zelda away.

☐ Horax and Zelda climb inside the rocket.

2 🛡 Imagine Horax and Zelda are at the police station. What do the police ask? Write questions.

Why are you following Ben and Lucy?

3 🖐 🛡 Read the story. What can we learn from it? Draw 😃 or 😣.

'Can we have fish for dinner, please?' Gan and his younger brother Li asked their mother. 'No, I'm sorry. Fish is too expensive,' she answered, 'but Gan, you can try to catch some in the lake.'

Gan went to the lake. He saw an old man fishing, but he didn't speak to him. Gan put some bread on the hook and started fishing. After two hours, he didn't have any fish and he decided to go home.

The next day, he went to the lake again. The old man was there again. This time Gan spoke to him. When Gan put some bread on the hook, the old man said, 'The fish in this lake don't like bread, I'll give you some corn.'

After two hours, Gan had five fish. 'Thank you very much,' he said to the old man. The old man smiled.

◯ Older people don't know anything.

◯ Older people can teach us things.

1 🎧 023 **Listen and write the missing words. Then say with a friend.**

Carl: Look at the ball!

Millie: We did it!

Carl: Yes. _____ _____

_____ _____ .

Millie: I'll be an astronaut one day!

Ryan: I've no idea how to get there.

Beth: Yes, it's a bit confusing, but

_____ _____

_____ .

Ryan: OK. First we need to find where we are.

Beth: Yes, and then we can see where we need to go.

2 **Look and write the words.**

farmer   driver   taller   smaller   clever   river   ~~teacher~~   waiter

teacher

_____   _____   _____   _____

3 🎧 024 **Listen, say and check your answers.**

1 **Read the text and choose the best answer. Lucas is talking to an alien.**

1 Lucas: Can you understand me?

    Alien: A ☑ Yes, I can.

            B ☐ Yes, I am.

            C ☐ Yes, I have.

2 Lucas: Where is your spaceship?

    Alien: A ☐ It's great.

            B ☐ It's behind the hill.

            C ☐ Here you are.

3 Lucas: When did you arrive?

    Alien: A ☐ Twelve o'clock is fine.

            B ☐ In front of the house.

            C ☐ An hour ago.

4 Lucas: Would you like to come to my house?

    Alien: A ☐ I like your house a lot.

            B ☐ Yes, please. I'd like to see it.

            C ☐ Yes, please. My house is great.

5 Lucas: Are you hungry?

    Alien: A ☐ Yes, please.

            B ☐ Yes, it is.

            C ☐ Yes, I am.

6 Alien: Have you got any cheese?

    Lucas: A ☐ Yes, I have.

            B ☐ Yes, I like it.

            C ☐ Yes, it does.

1 Look at the pictures and read the story. Write some words to complete the sentences about the story. You can use 1, 2 or 3 words.

A hot day in the mountains

Last July, my parents, my brother and I were on holiday in the mountains. One day, when Dad was driving on a mountain road, he suddenly stopped the car.

'Look,' he shouted. We all looked but no-one could see anything.

'I saw an alien, I'm sure. It went over that hill.'

We all got out of the car and started to walk up the hill.

1 Dad stopped the car on a __mountain road__.
2 Only Dad could see the _____ at first.
3 The alien went _____.

When we got to the top of the hill, we all saw the alien walk behind some rocks. It was small and green. We ran to the rocks, but when we got there, it wasn't there. We couldn't see it anywhere in the mountains.

'I'm sure the alien came here,' said Dad.

'I saw it too,' I said.

4 The alien walked _____.
5 The alien wasn't anywhere _____.

We walked back to the road, but now our car wasn't there. We walked to the nearest village and told our story to a police officer. 'I think we've got your car,' he said. He took us to the back of the police station and there was our car. We were very happy. 'And the alien?' asked Dad. 'Do you believe us?' We went inside and in the police station we saw two men. One of them was wearing an alien costume. 'This is your alien,' said the police officer, 'and this is his friend. While you were following the alien, his friend took your car.' They are robbers.

6 The family's car was at the _____.
7 One of the robbers was wearing _____.

Space

1 **Read the text about space. Answer the question.**

How many moons has Saturn got? _____

The sun is a big star in space. It is the only star we can see in the daytime. It is a very big star – we can put a million Earths in it! There are eight planets in the solar system. They all go around, or orbit, the sun. Earth takes 365 days to go around the sun. That is one year. Mars is further from the sun than Earth. This means it takes Mars 687 days to go around the sun. So, one year on Mars is 687 days!

Many planets have a moon too. A moon is small and it orbits a planet. It takes our moon 27 days to orbit Earth. Some planets have lots of moons – Saturn has 62 moons!

2 **Draw lines to make sentences.**

1 All the planets   a is longer than a year on Earth.

2 It takes one year   b a million times bigger than Earth.

3 A year on Mars   c a lot of moons.

4 The only star we can see   d go around the sun.

5 The sun is more than   e in the day is the sun.

6 Some planets have   f for a planet to orbit the sun.

3 **Read and write the correct word.**

the moon   Earth   Saturn   Mars   ~~the sun~~

1 It's a star. ___the sun___

2 It has 62 moons. _____

3 Its year is 687 days. _____

4 Its year is 365 days. _____

5 It orbits Earth. _____

4 **Read the fact file about the International Space Station. Answer the question.**

Why does it use the sun's energy? _____

The International Space Station

- The International Space Station (ISS) travels very fast. It orbits Earth every 90 minutes – that's 16 times a day!
- We can see the ISS in the night sky. It looks like a small circle.
- The ISS uses energy from the sun to work.
- Scientists study Biology, Physics, the planets and the weather in the ISS.
- The ISS has two bathrooms, a gym and six bedrooms. It has a big window and astronauts can see the planets and other objects in space.
- Astronauts from 15 different countries live and work on the ISS. They are strong because they exercise every day.
- The American astronaut Peggy Whitson lived and worked on the ISS for 665 days.

5 **Read and write _t_ (true) or _f_ (false).**

1 The ISS orbits Earth 16 times a day. [t]

2 We can see the ISS during the day. [ ]

3 Astronauts study things in the ISS. [ ]

4 They can't see space from the ISS. [ ]

5 The astronauts use the gym every day. [ ]

6 A woman astronaut lived on the ISS for more than one year. [ ]

6 **Imagine you are an astronaut in the ISS. Write about your day.**

In the morning, I _____.

_____

_____

1 🎧 025 **Put the dialogue in order. Then listen and check.**

☐ **A:** Hi, Gog. Nice to meet you. How old are you?

☐ **B:** I'm collecting rocks. It's my hobby – intergalactic rock-collecting. What about you? Have you got a hobby?

1 **A:** Hello, do you speak my language?

☐ **B:** I'm Gog.

☐ **A:** 45 languages. That's great. I'm Mary Franklin. What's your name?

☐ **B:** That would be great. I'd love to.

☐ **A:** I'm 12. Gog, tell me, what are you doing here on Earth?

☐ **B:** Yes, I do. I can understand you, Earth girl. I speak 45 languages.

☐ **A:** Yes, I collect badges. Would you like to see them?

☐ **B:** I'm 235 years old. How old are you, Mary?

2 **Look and write a dialogue. Use language from Activity 1.**

Alien: Hello, Earth boy.

Boy: _____

_____

_____

_____

_____

_____

1 Colour the bricks to make sentences. Write in the missing words and letters.

1	He did	you be	so I couldn't hear her.
2	She spoke	the exercise	when you grow up?
3	I'll	the old	vase careful____.
4	What _____	very quiet____,	one day.
5	Please clean	_____ famous	very bad ly .

2 Read and think. Then write two more sentences.

BIG QUESTION Why is space exciting?

There are many planets in space. _____

_____

_____

3 Read. Then write about you and draw.

When I grow up, I will be a _____
scientist. I will find new medicine _____
for sick people. _____

9 At the campsite

1 Write the words.

> put up   collect   ~~sail~~   make   make   swing on   row   dive into   dry

1 ___sail___ a boat
2 _____ wood
3 _____ a boat

4 _____ a rope
5 _____ the water
6 _____ a fire

7 _____ your clothes
8 _____ a raft
9 _____ a tent

2 Look and write sentences.

Jamie

1 __He's sailing a boat.__

Freya

2 _____

Paul

3 _____

Rebecca

4 _____

Marco

5 _____

Ruth

6 _____

Liam

7 _____

Sophie

8 _____

Matt

9 _____

3 Imagine you're going on a camping trip. Write three things you want to do there.

I want to _____, _____ and _____.

1 Look and write.

1 __some__ biscuits

2 __a packet of__ biscuits

3 _____ milk

4 _____ milk

5 _____ tomatoes

6 _____ tomatoes

7 _____ bread

8 _____ bread

2 Look and complete the dialogues.

1 A: Would you like __a packet of sweets__ ?

B: Yes, please.

2 A: Let's take _____ to the party.

B: That's a good idea.

3 A: Can I have _____, please?

B: Yes, of course. Chocolate cake or fruit cake?

3 Write a shopping list.

A packet of biscuits _____

A piece of _____

_____ _____

1 🛡 **Remember the song. Number the food.**

[ ] a can of tomatoes

[1] a loaf of bread

[ ] a can of tuna

[ ] a piece of cheese

[ ] a bottle of milk

[ ] a piece of meat

[ ] a packet of pasta

[ ] a bottle of sauce

2 🛡 **Imagine you are preparing dinner on a camping trip. Complete the verse. Then draw your meal.**

Pass me _____,

A _____ too,

_____, _____

And I'll make dinner for you.

3 **What's the problem? Read and draw lines.**

Pass me | a can of tomatoes, | some pasta | and a loaf of bread. | And I'll make lunch for you.

Oh, but ✗ ✗ ✗ , so I can't!

1 **Write *much* or *many*.**

1 How ____much____ cheese have we got?

2 How _____ eggs have we got?

3 How _____ apples have we got?

4 How _____ milk have we got?

5 How _____ bread have we got?

6 How _____ bottles of water have we got?

2 **Look at the picture. Answer the questions from Activity 1.**

1 We've got three pieces of cheese.

2 _____

3 _____

4 _____

5 _____

6 _____

3 **Imagine you need to buy some food. Write dialogues.**

1 A: How much chocolate do we need _____?

  B: We need four bars of chocolate. _____

2 A: _____ ?

  B: _____

3 A: _____ ?

  B: _____

4 A: _____ ?

  B: _____

4 bars of chocolate

2 carrots

a bottle of orange juice

4 bananas

1 Remember the story *The last line*. Match the sentence halves.

1 The children find the last line ⎯⎯⎯⎯⎯⎯⎯⎯⎯⎯⎯⎯⎯   a in order.

2 Then they put the rhyme   b behind a picture.

3 They go to the lighthouse   c in the newspaper.

4 The key which they need is   d under the floor.

5 Buster helps to find the chest   e on the beach.

6 Horax and Zelda read about it ⎯⎯⎯⎯⎯⎯⎯⎯⎯⎯   f on an oar.

2 Complete Ben and Lucy's story. Use two words from the box in each sentence.

> dragon ring conductor accident restaurant rocket door map car
> train treasure ~~shield~~ trumpet lighthouse trap man ~~knight~~ tunnel

1 Lucy and Ben <u>find the first line on the knight's shield</u> .

2 Horax tries to steal _____ .

3 Grandpa helps a man who has _____ .

4 When _____ , Lucy takes the tickets.

5 Grandpa wanted to catch a _____ who had _____ with *H* on it.

6 Horax and Zelda _____ the children _____ .

7 When Horax sees _____ , he puts the map _____ .

8 Ben and Lucy play a trick and close _____ .

9 They find _____ .

3 Write the lines of the rhyme in order.

There's the key to end this game.

    Climb more stairs and look out west.

In the lighthouse, you will see

    Behind the picture in the frame

Lots of stairs. Climb thirty-three!

    Look down and find the treasure chest.

In the lighthouse, you will see
_____
_____
_____
_____
_____
_____
_____

1 🎧 **026** **Listen and write the missing words. Then say with a friend.**

1

Mum: So Esme, what do you think?

Esme: Well, erm, _____
_____ beautifully.

Mum: Yes, I know. But is it nice?
Come on, tell me.

Esme: Erm, it's horrible, Mum.

2

Kate: OK, so where are we?

Chris: I'm not sure. But I think we're
quite close now.

Kate: But _____
_____ do we have to go?

Chris: Erm, I don't know.

2 **Look and write the words. You can use the words more than once.**

bottle   can   loaf   packet   piece   cup

1 a ___**cup**___ of tea   2 a _____ of crisps   3 a _____ of bread

4 a _____ of cake   5 a _____ of lemonade   6 a _____ of chocolate

7 a _____ of peas   8 a _____ of biscuits   9 a _____ of water

3 🎧 **027** **Listen, say and check your answers.**

1 Read the camping story again and circle.

1 (Mum) / Dad wants to go camping.

2 Dad prefers **camping** / **hotels**.

3 Mum makes a list of the **flowers** / **things** they need.

4 The family spends **the first day of** / **all of** their holiday in the camping shop.

5 Mum **takes everything outside** / **puts everything in the car.**

6 It takes **two hours** / **half an hour** to get to the campsite.

2  Imagine you are going camping. Make a list of ten things you are going to take with you. Circle the most important thing.

umbrella
_____
_____
_____

3 Imagine you forgot the most important thing on your list. What do you do?

_____
_____
_____

4 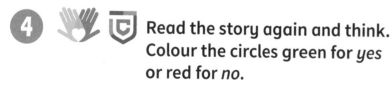 Read the story again and think. Colour the circles green for *yes* or red for *no*.

◯ It's good to prepare carefully before an important event.

◯ You can get ready for an important event just before it happens.

1 🎧 028 **Listen and draw lines.**

Jane   Vicky   Paul   Fred

Jack   Daisy   Sally

MEASUREMENTS

1 How do we measure these things? Look and write the questions.

> How wide is it?   ~~How long is it?~~   How heavy is it?   How high is it?

 **1**    **2** 10 KG    **3**    **4**

How long is it?   _____   _____   _____

2 Read the fact file. Why is it important to measure things? Read and tick ☑.

☐ **A** Because it's fun.

☐ **C** To help our parents.

☐ **B** It helps us prepare for everyday things.

WHY DO WE MEASURE THINGS?

Doctors and our parents measure our height and weight. They do this to help see how healthy we are. And it's fun to know how much we grow. We also measure things in Science and Maths. This helps us to learn more about our world. But we also measure lots of other things at home and outside every day!

We measure time. We mustn't be late for school. So we measure how long it takes us to get to school by car, bus, bike or on foot. What about TV programmes? We look at the clock and measure time, so we don't miss our favourite programmes!

When we are ill, we take medicine to get better. But how much medicine do we take? A lot of medicine is very bad for you. We measure medicine, so we have just enough to get well.

Too much sugar or flour in a cake won't taste nice. A lot of pepper in food is too hot! But if we measure things we put in food, it tastes just right.

3 **Read the fact file again. Write *t* (true) or *f* (false).**

1 Doctors measure our weight to see if we are healthy. `t`

2 We measure time, so we know when things start and finish. ☐

3 Our favourite TV programmes help us measure time. ☐

4 We must measure medicine to make sure we get better. ☐

5 A lot of medicine is good for you. ☐

6 We measure things, so our food tastes good. ☐

4 **What measurements are important in these pictures? Look and circle.**

time / distance   size / weight   temperature / weather

5 **Think about your day. What two things did you measure? Write and draw.**

1 Match the questions and answers.

1 What are your holiday plans, Charlotte?

2 Where do they live?

3 And what are you going to do there?

4 What are you going to do afterwards?

5 Are you going to stay in a hotel?

6 So are you going to swim all day?

a No, we're going to stay at a campsite near the sea.

b In the first week of the holidays, I'm going to visit my grandparents.

c After that, I'm going to France with my parents.

d No, I'm going to learn to surf. My mum is going to teach me.

e In Ireland.

f My grandparents have a farm and I'm going to look after the dogs and the pony.

2 Look at Activity 1. Underline the mistakes. Then write the correct sentences.

Charlotte is going to visit her <u>uncle and aunt</u>. They have a hotel in Spain. She's going to look after the cows. Then she's going to France with her brother. She's going to build sandcastles all day. In France, Charlotte is going to stay at a hotel.

Charlotte is going to visit her grandparents.

_____

_____

_____

_____

3 Write about your holiday plans.

This summer, I'm going

What do I know?

1 Look and draw lines to make sentences.

1 How

little	bread	do we	need?
much	eggs	are we	needs?
many	egg	are there	needing?

2 Pass

him	a piece	of bread,	thanks.
me	a loaf	of cake,	please.
us	a packet	of crisps,	please?

3 How

many	milk	we have got	on the table?
much	chocolate	have we got	next to the chair?
old	books	we have	in the fridge?

BIG QUESTION What do we know about camping?

2 Read and think. Then write two more sentences.

We put up a tent and make a fire.
_____
_____

About me!

3 Read. Then write about you and draw.

I'm going on a picnic today. I'm going to take a bag of crisps, a bottle of orange juice and some sandwiches.

My Super Mind

1 **In the museum**

Colour your favourite lessons.

singing the song

reading *The Explorers'* story

reading *Family stories*

learning about timelines

acting out our museum cat play

writing an advert

Word focus — Write three new words.

_____ _____ _____

Language focus — Write two sentences about yourself.

_____

_____

Now tell a friend what you like and don't like in Unit 1.

---

2 **The world around us**

Colour your favourite lessons.

singing the song

reading *The Explorers'* story

learning about maps and satellites

finding out about our free time

writing about my favourite outdoor place

Word focus — Write three new words.

_____ _____ _____

Language focus — Write two sentences about yourself.

_____

_____

Now tell a friend what you like and don't like in Unit 2.

---

3 **Danger!**

Colour your favourite lessons.

singing the song

reading *The Explorers'* story

reading *Danger on the beach*

learning about floods

acting out our emergency services play

writing a story about an accident

Word focus — Write three new words.

_____ _____ _____

Language focus — Write two sentences about yourself.

_____

_____

Now tell a friend what you like and don't like in Unit 3.

4 Two return tickets

Colour your favourite lessons.

singing the song

reading *The Explorers'* story

learning about ways to travel

acting out our ticket office play

writing a notice for a school board

Write three new words.

_____ _____ _____

Write two sentences about yourself.

_____

_____

Now tell a friend what you like and don't like in Unit 4.

---

5 Police!

Colour your favourite lessons.

singing the song

reading *The Explorers'* story

reading *The Gentleman Robber*

learning about sketches

finding out about our reading habits

writing a book review

Write three new words.

_____ _____ _____

Write two sentences about yourself.

_____

_____

Now tell a friend what you like and don't like in Unit 5.

---

6 Mythical beasts

Colour your favourite lessons.

singing the song

reading *The Explorers'* story

learning about dinosaurs

acting out our unusual animal play

drawing and writing about an imaginary beast

Write three new words.

_____ _____ _____

Write two sentences about yourself.

_____

_____

Now tell a friend what you like and don't like in Unit 6.

7 Orchestra practice

Colour your favourite lessons.

- singing the song
- reading *Tristan and the triangle*
- finding out about music in our class
- reading *The Explorers'* story
- learning about instrument families
- writing about my favourite band or singer

Word focus Write three new words.

_____ _____ _____

Language focus Write two sentences about yourself.

_____

_____

Now tell a friend what you like and don't like in Unit 7.

---

8 In the planetarium

Colour your favourite lessons.

- singing the song
- learning about space
- writing a space diary entry
- reading *The Explorers'* story
- acting out our interview with an alien

Word focus Write three new words.

_____ _____ _____

Language focus Write two sentences about yourself.

_____

_____

Now tell a friend what you like and don't like in Unit 8.

---

9 At the campsite

Colour your favourite lessons.

- singing the song
- reading *Let's go camping!*
- finding out about our holiday plans
- reading *The Explorers'* story
- learning about measurements
- writing a holiday leaflet

Word focus Write three new words.

_____ _____ _____

Language focus Write two sentences about yourself.

_____

_____

Now tell a friend what you like and don't like in Unit 9.